Parables of PIGS:
People
In
God's
Service

Biographies and Reflections
of a Modern Missionary

Jacqueline Nairnsey-Sayles

jnairnsey@yahoo.com

First U.S. Edition.
Nairnsey-Sayles, Jacqueline

Parables of PIGS/by Jacqueline Nairnsey-Sayles
ISBN-13: 978-0-9761256-1-7 (Miracle Mission Press)

Cover Design by Holly Pituch of Clever Girl Marketing
Edited by Megan LaFollett of Meraki Editing & Julie Gabell

"He said to them, 'Go into all the world and preach the good news to all creation.'"

Mark 16:15 (NIV)

This book is dedicated to the Children of Casa Hogar, City of Hope in Honduras, who will make a huge difference to their country and their culture – each child is a true light of God's promises.

And to:

Charlie, Robbie, Max, Sam, Josh, and Timothy, the dearest and most wonderful grandsons imaginable.

TABLE OF CONTENTS

Acknowledgements

First and foremost I have a list of folk who have been praying over me and this book for more than a year – you know who you are! Friends at CBS both in Tampa and in Houston, Bible study friends at Kingsland Baptist, virtually everyone at my beloved Cypress Point Community Church, and mission teams from Community Wesleyan Church, Rockledge Presbyterian Church and the fabulous Grow Life Church in Wesley Chapel. Without your love and prayers, there would be no *Parables of Pigs*.

Secondly, I would like to thank all those brave missionaries who agreed to let me add their life's journey to these pages, and in the process enriched the substance and content.

Next I have my amazing editors – Megan LaFollett in Houston who virtually pulled the whole thing together, and was a constant encouragement and a relentless source of great ideas; and dear Julie Gabell in the Tampa area, who edited my last book and massaged a lot of the parables in this one.

There is a long list of "angels" who support my mission trips financially, and love me unconditionally. You are the unsung heroes of my missions. I need to mention two (although they will hate it): Wanda Smith and Kristine Sage in Palm Beach County.

Now we have The Tea Room Ladies...Carole Stephens, Tina Wilkens, and Kristen Heath. We are the Four Musketeers and I love you guys!

I have the two most amazing son-in-laws, Jody Licatino and Rob Piccirilli (Pickles). Both godly men who encourage, love, and generously share their considerable insight and wisdom. They support me in every way possible.

Most important of all are my two daughters Abigail and Vicki, the most amazing women of God, whose unconditional love, perception and discernment are priceless.

Hymn of a Missionary: Your Eyes to See

Please give me Lord, your eyes to see
The need, the pain, the poverty.
Children running streets alone,
No place to sleep or call their home.
Children who are left unshod;
They need you Lord; they need my God.

Please give me Lord your eyes to see
The lack of love, the misery.
Your families ripped apart in pain
By drink, by drugs, for other's gain.
Dear families, who in darkness plod,
They need you Lord; they need my God.

Please give me Lord your eyes to see
Those lands of bondage far from me.
People who in prison pray
For peace, for joy, for freedom's day.
Desperate folk who know no love;
They need you Lord; they need my God.

Please give me Lord your eyes to see
What I must learn to be like thee.
Please give your strength and give your wealth
Of wisdom, knowledge and yourself.
Instill in me your truth and Word
I need you Lord; I need my God.

FOREWORD

BY OMAR C. GARCIA | MISSIONS PASTOR
KINGSLAND BAPTIST CHURCH | KATY, TEXAS

I HAVE LOVED STORIES all my life. My grandfather told me of a runaway slave named Androcles and the kindness that he showed to a lion with an injured paw. That story not only stirred my imagination, it taught me a lesson that I have never forgotten about the value of demonstrating kindness to others. The story of Androcles and the Lion was only the first of many stories I enjoyed as a child.

I not only gleaned practical wisdom from stories, I also learned about my own family history by listening to stories. In the days before we had television, I would listen to my grandparents talk on the front porch of their home in the evenings. They told and retold lots of interesting stories, some dating back generations, about our family. These stories provided the context that helped me understand my own life and where I fit into the grander scheme of our family history.

Our lives are, essentially, a collection of stories — the personal accounts, however mundane or exciting, of our days. If you want to get to know someone well, then listen carefully to their stories. Ask questions that prompt the telling of stories. Stories are the keys that give us access to the innermost parts of a person's heart. They bring clarity and promote understanding about the people we know and those we only know about from a distance.

The book you are holding in your hands is a collection of stories, more specifically, stories about people in God's service. My friend Jackie is more than a collector and writer of good stories, she is a steward of the stories that have come to her. She not only understands the value of caring for these stories, she knows the importance of giving them away. For some, a particular story may be the spark that ignites a passion or sets them on a new and unexpected course.

The stories that Jackie has written and collected will make you smile, cause you to reflect, and hopefully inspire you to find your place in God's story. Through them, Jackie encourages us to play an active role in the divine narrative of bringing glory to God among the nations. Her modern-day parables illustrate how our own lives can be interwoven with the grander story of God's love and pursuit of His creation.

Mother Teresa understood the importance of being a part of God's story. She said, "I am a little pencil in the hand of a writing God who is sending a love letter to the world." What an amazing opportunity we have to be a part of that love story. Our own lives are enriched in proportion to how much we allow God to write His love story through us. May we willingly submit to His hand and allow Him to guide our movements so that what is left when we are gone is a beautiful story that will continue to inspire others.

One day, our story will come to an end. And when we die, we will do so "in medias res," a Latin phrase that means "in the middle of a story." The good news is that although our stories will come to an end, God's story will continue to be written by those who come after us. May the stories in this book inspire you to love and serve God and to become a dynamic part of His divine narrative.

PREFACE

A DECADE AGO, I moved up to Tampa from West Palm Beach, and with much trepidation started to write a book. It took over two years to complete, and in all honesty I should have given myself even more time to find the hundreds of small mistakes that remained when I inflicted it on the public. I had reached the stage, however, where I knew if I didn't take the plunge and get it published, it would never happen. Once I held the finished "masterpiece" in my hands, I breathed a huge sigh of relief, thinking that God would now release me from His insistence that I write. He did!

That is until about two years ago, when the incessant prompting started again. Much like the first time, I tried to ignore His urging and nudging. I used many of the same excuses and posed the same challenges: lack of talent, lack of funds, not seeing the purpose, not having the time. So I managed to postpone the inevitable decision to write for at least a year.

"Okay Lord, what is it that You want me to write about?" I finally asked during one of my daily, early morning conversations.

In my months of avoidance and denial, I had considered several options. Perhaps *Tales from a Tea Room*, sharing some of the wonderful, diverse stories from the five years I owned and ran Maggie's Tea Room in New Tampa. Maybe *Memories of a Missionary*, a compilation of experiences and stories from recent missionary trips – or even a short story devotional for those about to embark into the wonderful world of missions.

As often happens when I ask pointed questions in prayer, my answer did not come immediately. But as waiting on the Lord had become one of my favorite mantras, I settled happily into a delightful life of "loving on" my precious families in Tampa, Miami and Houston; fund raising for missions; and helping to build a new two story dormitory while spending time with the children at the City of Hope in Honduras. A couple of visits to help with construction projects at Mission Del Mar near La Ceiba kept my days full of work and joy, and I managed to hide the truth that I was secretly hoping to be released from the "writing" obligation.

Though I knew it was coming, I was still shocked when the marching orders arrived in the middle of a deep sleep on the bottom bunk at the City of Hope mission house. I woke up with a start, and there it was: Present Day Parables of PIGS...reflections of a missionary journey. Then, as with every other instruction I have been given by the Lord, it was confirmed by a series of

"God-incidences" (secularly called coincidences) being thrown at me from all directions. Of course, having had what I was to write confirmed, I then came to realize that many of the notes, stories, experiences and journaling I'd done over the prior year immediately became relevant to the new book. Without my seeing it, the Lord had allowed me to start on His book from the moment I had obeyed His call.

Although my worldly side constantly wonders who on earth might want to read the book, or perhaps even enjoy it, I know without any shadow of doubt that these questions are irrelevant. It is truly not my concern, nor for my benefit, but purely something that the Lord will use to and for His purpose, as He did with the first one. I do pray however, that I get the spiritual guidance, joy and fulfillment that I experienced from writing *The Power of Present Day Parables*, and that it might encourage and inspire others to step out in faith and to follow their own path to become a missionary.

The Bible teaches that it is not in our power to convert or open people's mind to Christ. That, I am relieved to say, is a "God Job" and a true and awesome gift given by Him[1]. I have come to understand that pride, coupled with a great deal of left brain thinking, can make it close to impossible for some folk to release what (they think) they know, in order to be open to the possibility that there may be another, better answer to life's

---

[1] *"For by Grace you have been saved through faith. And this is not your own doing: it is a gift of God"*. Ephesians 2:8 ESV

most important questions. It is the incessant indoctri-
nation from birth that *we* should have the answers, that
we need to be the one in charge, the leader, the winner,
the "all-knowing", that is the culprit. This makes it so
very difficult to let go of our precious and brilliant "self"
long enough to realize that we might not know it all,
and perhaps aren't meant to! I speak from
experience...can you tell?

We can add to this the fact that we are constantly
fed half-truths that lead us into a comfortable, acceptable, feasible, and yet false belief. Fortunately the truth is
not a secret, hidden away for the elite or the chosen. The
truth is found in the Bible, which has been around for
over two thousand years and easily available to much of
the world for the last century. Once you find the truth,
it will give you strength, understanding, self-worth, and
it *will* set you free[2].

Thus when it comes to truth and the relevancy of the
parable stories in this book, we will not be going to look
for answers on Google, in Bing, use Yahoo or in fact
anything on the internet. Neither will we be looking at
government documents, school manuals, or scholastic
theses. We will be gleaning our parable truth and
answers directly from the source.

---

[2] *"To the Jews who had believed in him, Jesus said, 'If you hold to
my teaching, you are really my disciples. Then you will know the
truth, and the truth will set you free".* John 8: 31-32 NIV

It is necessary for us all to acknowledge the stories of our lives. Yours are just as significant and important as mine. When we reflect back on our stories we can recognize mistakes, triumphs, reasons and consequences. However, much like the Bible itself, it is only by using what we learn in order to influence our future, that our stories bestow their greatest gift. So I write this book in the hope that it encourages you to write down your own experiences, search for parables in the Bible, and reflect on what you have been taught by them. Then try to use and repeat the successes, and attempt to avoid the mistakes.

Finally, my prayer for you is that you embrace with joy and gratitude every minute of your greatest gift from God—your life, the stories that encompass it, and more importantly, His son Jesus Christ who He sacrificed so we can all enjoy eternal life with Him.

– Jackie

"May your roots go down deep into the soil of God's marvelous love... and may you be able to feel and understand as all God's children should, how long and how wide and how deep and how high His love really is... so that, at last, you will be filled up to capacity with God himself."

Ephesians 3: 17-19 (TLB)

CHAPTER 1: PARABLE OF PERSPECTIVE

"The world is round and the place that may seem like the end might only be the beginning." {Ivy Baker Priest}

ONE OF THE MOST amazing phenomena we can encounter, and yet take for granted every day, is the ability to have different perspectives. The exact same incident, event, scene, experience, but seen from a different angle. And understood all the better when more than one perspective is taken into account.

We are all familiar with having different points of view, but there are few of us that can truly say that we seek to see things from another's perspective. This is for many reasons; the primary one being pride. After all, we are and need to be "right", don't we? Been there, done that!

A second cause is a very understandable desire to stay in a comfort zone. We are so much happier and relaxed to know what we know, believe what we want to believe, feel what we feel, and see things as we want to see them.

The third explanation may be, simply put, ignorance. Believe it or not, there are some folk around that don't even think there might be another perspective; sadly, I've been there and done that, too!

The greatest change in perspective I have personally experienced is my perception of who or what a Christian is. I had formed a less than attractive opinion of the species when I was nine years old, having been the victim of incorrect doctrine in an environment that had been thrust upon me and that I couldn't control.

Between the ages of nine and forty five, I managed to enlarge on my resentment, adding one criticism onto another, to the point that I could be considered aggressive in my hatred of Christians; especially those that considered themselves "born again". Living in a very secular environment, as most of us do, I bought into the opinion that Christians were very weak; that they had to rely on a power other than their own in order to succeed. What losers! On top of which, they felt that something written two thousand years ago could be relevant to our lives today...how out of touch can you get?

My amazement and contempt grew with the knowledge that these "losers" found it necessary to give a tenth of their income to their churches. Money is hard enough for most of us to earn; why in the world would you then give such a large portion away for someone else's benefit? After all, "charity begins at home", doesn't it?

Christ seemed merely a crutch to me. Something folk needed to lean on in times that they couldn't handle for themselves. And what about those difficult times; the death of a child, a husband, a best friend; what of sickness, injury, pain, and depression; the unfairness of war, genocide, natural disasters; would a loving God really allow all that to happen?

What hypocrites those Christians seemed to be, telling us not to sin, to obey the Ten Commandments, to love one another. They should take a good look at themselves...*they* are certainly not sin free. They aren't close to obeying the Ten Commandments; they kill, they envy, they commit adultery, they abuse those around them, and they even fight amongst themselves. The following passage shows much of what I felt:

I will live my life according to these beliefs
God does not exist
It's just foolish to think
That there is an all-knowing God with a cosmic plan
That an all-powerful God brings purpose to the pain and
suffering in the world
It's a comforting thought, however
It's only wishful thinking
People can do as they please
without eternal consequences
The idea that
I am deserving of hell,
Because of sin
Is a lie meant to make me a slave to those in power,
"The more you have, the happier you will be"
Our existence has no grand meaning or purpose,
In a world with no God
There is freedom to be who I want to be,
But with God
Life is an endless cycle of guilt and shame
Without God
Everything is fine
It is ridiculous to think
I am lost and in need of saving.

In all honesty, I know that I would still have that same perception of Christians had it not been for God taking the initiative and opening my eyes to Him; purely, I feel in hindsight, because of the pleas and prayers of Christian friends that surrounded me. There are certain of us, like the Apostle Paul and Jackie Sayles, who for a multitude of reasons would have remained in a world of oblivion had God, in His mercy, not taken matters into His own hands. The expression "eternal gratitude" takes on a whole new meaning!

Originally, the Apostle Paul was Saul of Tarsus; his change of name marks the time of his change in perspective. Saul was an incredibly intelligent and very well educated Pharisee who felt that the early followers of Christ were blasphemers of the Lord God of Israel. It took God's direct intervention in his life for him to re-examine his thoughts and come to the conclusion that Jesus was in fact the Messiah, Son of God. And that by killing and persecuting His followers, Paul was truly persecuting the Lord God of Israel, who he loved and wanted to serve.

God's Bible is a book full of different perspectives, gifted to us to increase our understanding of Him and the world as it truly is. Perhaps that is sometimes why so many of us become convicted by it. Some of us grow by that conviction. Some of us shy away from it. And some of us purely just don't want to believe it!

How many of us are honest enough to admit that we truly relate more to Martha than Mary[1], or to the son who had stayed home loyally working for his father instead of the prodigal son who squandered his inheritance[2]? How many of us would make

---

[1] Luke 10:38-42
[2] Luke 15:11-32

the decision to stick with the ninety nine sheep instead of risking all of them to look for the one who had strayed[3]? Am I the only one who can't understand how you can befriend, love and spend three precious years of your life teaching a man that you KNOW is going to betray you? Don't you wish that Jesus had just "dumped" Judas when He had the chance?

The gospel of John, chapter eight, is another example of a change in perspective. Jesus has been teaching in the temple and is leaving when a group of scribes and Pharisees throw a woman to the ground in front of him, saying that she had been caught in the act of adultery; according to the Hebrew laws this was punishable with death by stoning. They ask Jesus how he would handle this crime, hoping to catch him by going against the law to save her. Jesus isn't fazed; he kneels and writes in the sandy soil and then turns to the pious, vengeful men and suggests, "Let him who is without sin among you be the first to throw a stone at her." He then continues to write in the dirt as each of the men, one by one, turn and walk away[4].

This occurrence in Jesus' life serves to show us how significant a shift in perception can be. Here it meant the difference between life and death. Jesus had managed with a few words to convict a mob intent on killing a woman of sin and change them into individual men who could perceive and acknowledge their own sin, guilt, and shame. Suddenly these men were able to see with God's perspective, the truth that we are all sinners; and not one of us any better than anyone else.

---

[3] Luke 15:3-7
[4] John 8:1-10

INSTEAD OF CRITICIZING CHRISTIANS FOR BEING SINNERS, I NOW STRUGGLED AS A CHRISTIAN SINNER.

This event in the Bible played a significant role in changing my perception of Christians, because I hadn't truly ever considered myself as a sinner or needing forgiveness. In retrospect, I feel that this fact – not realizing our own sin and the need for forgiveness – is the basic reason that the secular world remains secular. We either don't see what we do or say as being a sin, or we feel that it is less of a sin than most others are committing! The majority of us feel that, if there is a heaven, there must be a "pass mark" in order to get there, and that in comparison to others we should be okay. Maybe we might benefit by "being graded on a curve"; or granted a second chance to take the exam, perhaps.

Having accepted the concept that much of what I did was a sin, I began to realize that becoming a Christian didn't seem to automatically stop it! In fact I became more and more aware of how much sin I had in my life. Becoming a Christian was by no means a comfortable change to my life, as pride was and still is a major vice that I struggle with. None of us like to be wrong, but I had also been very verbal in my dislike of Christians in the past. I had delighted in the fact they were weak, unintelligent idiots and hypocrites who needed a man called Jesus Christ as a "crutch" when they were in trouble – and now I was one of them. My need for a savior, someone to present himself to God on my behalf grew greater. Instead of criticizing Christians for being sinners, I now struggled as a Christian sinner.

The more I read and understood the Bible, the more I acknowledged the timeless nature of the truths, wisdom and guidance it gives. There didn't seem to be any issue that came up in my life, and still doesn't, that the Bible didn't address. Instead of regarding it as an ancient and irrelevant book, it became the essential "go-to" manual for my life. I found myself constantly bringing all my challenges, fears, heartbreaks, dreams, worries and everything that seemed to be going on in my life to lay at the feet of Jesus – after all, isn't that what He tells us to do in His Word?

He didn't just become a crutch for me; He became my hospital bed, along with the surgeon to operate and the nurse to make me well again. I can now truthfully say:

> *I am lost and in need of saving*
> *It is ridiculous to think*
> *Everything is fine*
> *Without God*
> *Life is an endless cycle of guilt and shame*
> *But with God*
> *There is freedom to be who I want to be*
> *In a world with no God*
> *Our existence has no grand meaning or purpose,*
> *"The more you have the happier you will be"*
> *Is a lie meant to make me a slave to those in power,*
> *Because of sin*
> *I am deserving of hell,*
> *The idea that*
> *People can do as they please*

without eternal consequences
Is only wishful thinking
It's a comforting thought, however
That an all-powerful God brings purpose
to the pain and suffering in the world
That there is an all-knowing God with a cosmic plan
It's foolish to think
God does not exist
I will live my life according to these beliefs.

Perhaps you recognize the words...the exact same ones written a couple of pages back to describe how I felt as a non-Christian, but now seen from a different perspective. In fact it is a word perfect reversal. What I felt about Christians, all their weaknesses, their beliefs in an ancient book, their sinning, their arguments, not being able to keep their own commandments, being hypocrites...none of it had changed, only my perception. And yes, I have each of those sins and vices, plus a great deal more!

When I first became a Christian, I was filled with regret that it hadn't happened earlier in my life. I seemed to be so behind in my knowledge of the Bible and knowing how to apply God and His truths to my life. Now I sincerely look back on the timing as a blessing. Not only do I get to truly appreciate the opportunity, love and caring that He showed to someone who was less than complimentary about Him, and recognize the incredible gift He gave me, but it has allowed me to be understanding and non-judgmental of those who have yet to see the world from a Christian perspective.

In other words, I get to see both sides of the equation. It helps me genuinely understand and see the secular world from another point of view. It is *only* through His Grace that I was saved myself; I am hardly in a position to be critical of others who haven't as yet seen the light.

As a missionary I get to share the Lord with many folk of other religions and beliefs. Some are receptive, some aren't. The great commission is to go out into the entire world to share the gospel of Christ, and I like to think I do this with my usual gusto; however, if someone comes to understand and accept Christ into their hearts I know that it has been God who opened their eyes, and I was merely the vessel He used.

Once their hearts have been opened, another of our Lord's greatest commands comes into play. Hebrews 12:15 says, "See to it that no one fails to obtain the grace of God." It should be understood and is significant that the Christian community is responsible for the individual's advancement in grace. We are not to abandon a recent convert, but help each to "grow" in faith.

I love my life as a missionary, because it shows me daily a little more of God's world, what is important to Him, what He wants me to see and understand, and how I might be able to help His hurting people; or in other words, to show me a little bit more of His perspective.

For my thoughts are not your thoughts,
neither are your ways my ways, declares the Lord.
For as the heavens are higher than the earth,
so are my ways higher than your ways and my
thoughts than your thoughts. Isaiah 55: 8-9 (ESV)

Back Row (left to right): Jackie Sayles, Steve Deardoff, Dean Reule, Bill Owens, Joyce Owens, Ted Hillstad, Ryan Coberly, David Harris
Front row: Hettie Reule, Grace Anne Reule, Eva Lopez, Renea Harris

CHAPTER 2: PARABLE OF THE PIGS

"As you get to know the men who walked with Jesus, you'll see that if He can accomplish his purpose through them, He can do the same through you." {John MacArthur}

THE NUMBER TWELVE has always been a favorite of mine. Mostly because it is so easily divisible, but also because it seems to have significance in so many of life's stories – perhaps the greatest being the New Testament account of the twelve disciples. Twelve totally diverse characters drawn together by one man who calls them to follow Him. He then totally changes their concept of life, teaches them, trains them, and finally sends them off to spread the Gospel to the world. In the process, these men would be horribly persecuted, tortured, and in some cases, even killed for their beliefs.

Yet to me, the most amazing part is that these particular twelve men were ever chosen by Jesus in the first place. They were everyday folk: fishermen, a political zealot, a hated tax collector, and other ordinary people like you and me. They most certainly weren't the saints (and would hate to think of themselves as such) we now see portrayed in stained glass windows. As John MacArthur puts it, they were "a bunch of regular guys". They were weak, prone to mistakes, remarkably unremarkable, and 100% human.

Prior to my very first mission trip in July of 2011, Renea Harris, our fearless mission leader, held two or three meetings to introduce the mission team to each other and to the basic nuances of being a short term missionary in order to arm us with the necessary advice and tools. Being a memory-challenged individual, I remember little of the details. But I do remember wondering who it was that was actually going, as the faces seemed different at each meeting.

Much of the reason for this, of course, might have been that I didn't honestly feel I was going until the final meeting, so I wasn't paying full attention. The group that eventually met at Tampa airport around 6 a.m. on July 2nd had only four individuals I knew personally: Pastor Dean, his wife Hettie, daughter Anne Grace, and Renea. I was getting over the effects of laryngitis, not feeling great, and not wanting to spread any errant germs, so I decided to remain remote from the rest of the team as much as possible with the knowledge that I would have plenty of time to get to know everyone later. Eleven of us boarded the flight to Miami. While we were awaiting the flight to San Pedro Sula we were joined by Steve from Indiana, who brought our number to twelve.

When we arrived at Mission Del Mar, we sat down with Scott Ledford and were introduced to the "do's and don'ts" of the establishment. Over the next seven days I had the privilege of getting to know the rest of our team, most of them members of the Christian Motorcycle Association (CMA). Their particular mission was to deliver ten brand new Honda motor bikes to local Honduran pastors who would otherwise have no mode of transportation to reach the remote regions of their mountainous parishes. Much like the original twelve disciples, however, this seemed to be the only point of daily life any of the group shared.

Renea Harris is a former nursing director for a home health agency, who now devotes most of her time and energy to finding ways in which to serve in missions and organize teams. David, Renea's husband, is what every small boy wants to be when he grows up: a firefighter. He is based out of the local Zephyrhills fire station.

Ryan is a mechanic working for Toyota in Pinellas; a young man aspiring to convert his private pilot's license to that of instructor. (I'm happy to report, something he has attained since his most recent mission trip in March of 2012.)

Bill and Joyce are married. After twenty-six years in the army, Joyce now works for The State of Florida in the department of finance and is one of the most talented artists that I know, with her work displayed in the local gallery in Plant City. Her husband Bill worked as a mechanic in the army for twenty-three years but is now retired.

Ted is also retired but had been working in a steel mill for thirty years as a mechanic.

Dean and Hettie Reule are the pastors who lead Cypress Point Church; at the time, their daughter Grace Anne was in 12th grade and not yet eighteen.

We were proud to have Steve, who came to us from Indiana and who works for Subaru of America. Steve is one of the most energetic and giving men one can hope to know.

Eva Lopez was also a member of our Cypress Point Church, but I hadn't had the opportunity to meet her before our trip. What a delightful woman! She works in the local Home Depot in Tampa, but you could tell that her focus was her ever growing family of grandchildren – much like myself.

Our interpreter companion, Israel, was fresh out of college and eager to enter the world of missions. The laughter, love and joy that this young man brought to the equation were immeasurable and priceless.

We were quite a diverse bunch, to say the least, our only similarity being our love of God and the delicious food that we virtually inhaled each morning and evening. So much so that we managed to gain the dubious reputation of being "pigs".

Yet as we worked our way through the week-long mission, it became obvious that we were all meant to be there, each one needed and necessary for the multiple jobs and assignments that came to light. None of us were left with any doubt as to whether we were of use, as all our individual experiences and talents were utilized; we sang, we danced, we acted, we taught, we built crafts, catered snacks and lunches, we played games, sewed, cuddled, comforted, and delivered the message of the gospel.

IT DOESN'T MATTER WHO YOU ARE, HOW OLD YOU ARE, WHAT YOU DO, WHERE YOU COME FROM, OR WHAT YOUR EXPERIENCES MIGHT BE...GOD CAN, AND WILL, ALWAYS BE ABLE TO USE YOU FOR HIS SERVICE.

The CMA team cleaned and repaired motorcycles, cars, and vans that belonged to pastors from the surrounding area. They also stuffed plastic carrier bags with rice, beans and palm oil in their spare time, and we all were grateful to be taken to deliver these to poverty stricken families in the remote areas around the mission. Midweek we had the privilege to present the ten new Honda motorcycles donated by the CMA organization, at a thanksgiving service held in the local church. The total fleet of bikes CMA had donated in Honduras had reached seventy strong!

Renea had asked each of us to deliver a devotional for our Morning Prayer meetings and I was due to have mine prepared for the day after the motorcycle presentation. While reading my Bible and the book I had brought with me, *Twelve Ordinary Men* by John MacArthur, I recognized the parallels between the Disciples of Jesus and His disciples in our missionary team of hungry pigs. As there seemed to be a lot of the gospel written "around" eating events (three or four parables, three miracles, and the Last Supper), I can only imagine that the original twelve also had hearty appetites.

My devotional began to take shape around the premise of twelve ordinary, diverse characters being thrown together in the service of the Lord, all willing to step out of their comfort zones in order to obey the call of missions work. The most important insight being that it doesn't matter who you are, how old you are, what you do, where you come from, or what your experiences might be...God can, and will, always be able to use you for His service.

Suddenly the light turned on! We truly did all have something in common. Yes, we were indeed a happy band of P.I.G.S. – People In God's Service. I was excited to share the acronym and analogy to my group the next morning, knowing that our newly attained reputation could be put to good use and with a much better connotation.

The devotional on Thursday was received with hoots of laughter, which had of course been one of the objectives. Our little band of PIGS snorted and honked their way through the next couple of days, and I was rewarded with a beautifully painted ceramic pig given anonymously. Our resident artist, Joyce, painted the words "People In God's Service" on its rump, and we left it as a gift to the Ledfords who had fed us so very well at Mission Del Mar. Joyce then painted an exact replica of the pig and gave us all a postcard with the image on it. This image was also airbrushed onto the grey t-shirts that are now used for all our mission teams organized by Renea from Cypress Point Church.

Mine was of course not the only life to be changed by that mission trip to Honduras. Most of the first-time missionaries were deeply moved and affected, to the point of committing their life to mission work of some sort in the future. The veterans of our team had their previous commitments confirmed. I couldn't wait to get home to see my family and to tell them of my defined call to do more mission work, knowing that God would be instrumental in setting that in motion. He did...but that is another story and another parable!

"And he said to them, 'Go into all the world and proclaim the gospel to the whole creation'."
Mark 16:15 (NIV)

CHAPTER 3: PARABLE OF THE WALL PLAQUE

"Becoming an instrument of God's love is a slow process that requires that we allow God to use us to serve others one choice at a time. When we make ourselves available to God to use in this way (unconditional service), then each act of kindness becomes one more sentence in the narrative of our lives that makes our story worth reading." {Omar Garcia}

O NE OF THE MOST treasured gifts that I have given my daughter Vicki is a plaque that she put in her kitchen that says, "Ask not what your mother can do for you; ask what you can do for your mother."

This is, of course, a play on the famous words of John F. Kennedy. The plaque has been a source of laughter to family and guests for many years. It wasn't until recently, however, that I was challenged by an even better, more important version of JFK's words; a version that was to change my life and encourage me to take the next step in my Christian walk: "Ask not what God can do for you; ask what you can do for God."

Having just prayed and presented my daily list of wants and needs to God, I felt humbled and not just a little brainless! It wasn't a question of what and who I should put in my prayers, for I know without doubt that God wants us to bring all our pain, needs, hopes, and dreams directly to Him. He certainly wants to hear us tell Him who needs His help and intervention. No, it's not a matter of what we pray to the Lord; it's a matter of where our heart is.

Instead of asking the Lord to heal someone and then moving on to the next request, shouldn't I be asking if there is something I could do, or that He could enable me to do, to help with my request? Perhaps I should ask for the time to make a home or hospital visit; or in the event that I don't personally know the person in my prayers, to write a card of hope or encouragement. Or, if I am truly concerned and want God to help my friend get a job, shouldn't I be asking for someone or something to come into my own life to open up a door for them? It's so very easy to make a request, and then leave all the work to God. Yet if a miracle is needed, shouldn't I desire to be a part of that miracle?

Vicki's plaque serves to remind me where the main focus, not only of my prayers but also of my life, should be. My first mission trip to Honduras was the catalyst that shifted the focus of my prayers from God needing to service the needs as I saw them, to being able to see the needs from God's standpoint and being made a part of the solution.

One Sunday in September of 2010, my church announced an upcoming mission trip to Honduras in July; those who were interested were asked to stop by the mission table on the way out. I wasn't interested! Though I had always admired and supported missionaries, being a missionary had never been of interest to me. It most definitely was not on my "bucket list".

By the end of the service, God specifically spoke to me with instructions not only to visit the mission table, but also to fill in the application form. I have to admit I was a bit irritated as I stepped up to comply.

Application Questions and Answers:

Have you had any previous experience as a missionary?
   "No"

If so, what was your overall impression of the experience?
   ...blank!

Do you have any experience in teaching?
   "No"

What talents or craft skills do you feel you possess?
   ...blank!

Why do you want to go on this trip?
   ...blank! (though I was tempted to put "I don't!")

What do you hope to gain/achieve by going on this trip?
   "I have absolutely no idea!"

How do you think this trip might change your life?
   "I have absolutely no idea!"

Well, I couldn't be accused of dishonesty! The answers reflected exactly how I felt, and I was sure that one look at my form was all that it would take for it to be crumpled and trashed. So, I left Cypress Point Church confident that I needn't

AS USUAL, GOD WAS PREPARING THE PATH FOR ME LONG BEFORE HE ASKED ME TO WALK IT.

worry about the outcome. The fact that I ran a tearoom and couldn't spare the time or money wasn't ever going to be an issue.

It wasn't until the beginning of December that I discovered that I had been added to the list of folk going to Honduras. *Oh, bother.* Now I had to think about raising funds and organizing someone to take over my duties at the tearoom. This wasn't convenient at all! I asked for prayer, totally oblivious to the irony of my own prayers "to have God give me better ways of being His instrument".

Well, God started to answer my prayers by reorganizing my life! As usual, He was preparing the path for me long before He asked me to walk it.

Back in June, my daughter Vicki and her husband Pickles had asked me to live with them in their new home in Country Walk that had a mother-in-law suite upstairs. The fact that this house also had its own gorgeous pool and backed to a conservation area (fondly nicknamed "The Serengeti"), had made the decision to move there in August an easy one. My own little home in Heritage Isles had been leased by a friend and her family, and was close to paying its way.

By Christmas, my business partner Teresa and I had accepted the fact that we needed to close the tearoom. It was losing money by the day, and we had come to the end of our five-year lease. Trying to negotiate a new lease seemed fruitless. By the end of the year we made the agonizing decision to shut the doors of Miracles and Maggie's Tea Room at the end of March.

The opportunity of moving most of the tearoom catering equipment from the tearoom to just five doors north in the same Cory Lake Professional Center building, was more than convenient; but to be able to share a ready-made and licensed double kitchen facility with a gluten-free bakery in order to start and run a new catering business, was nothing short of a miracle. We managed to sell off most of the inventory at the store in order to pay down our only loan, and by the end of March, Teresa and I had just a small business debt left.

April marked my 65th birthday, Medicare, and the ability to retire if I so chose. Though I still sincerely felt that I would get a last minute reprieve from the missionary obligation, funds came in from friends and family for the Cypress Point mission trip in July. God had me "covered" in every part of my life!

I spent April, May, and June starting up the new catering business, establishing new menus, a website, and clientele. By the beginning of July, I was in a situation where a week away was not going to devastate me financially, and though still trying to get over the effects of a summer cold and laryngitis, I felt at peace leaving for Honduras on July 2, 2011.

I was truly only acquainted with four out of the twelve in our team, comprised of six folk from our church, five from the Christian Motorcycle Association (CMA), and Steve Deardoff, a lone mission traveler who joined us in Miami. Our mission was to run a Vacation Bible Study for the local children, help with an outreach feeding station, and deliver ten new motor-cycles (donated by CMA) to pastors in and around La Ceiba. We also planned to set up a week-long maintenance station for the local missionaries, volunteers, and pastors who couldn't afford to have their vehicles repaired or serviced.

We arrived at Mission Del Mar, our final destination, at 10 p.m. local time. Though worn out from the long journey, I slept very little that first night. I was not used to the cacophony of noise: dance music from three local bars, the competing bark-ing of dogs, rooster calls, and snores of my companions that rendered my newly acquired ear plugs completely useless. At 5:00 a.m. I was bombarded with yet another onslaught of noise—a real "dawn chorus." Thousands upon thousands of birds awakened in the trees surrounding Mission Del Mar, and for me they gave new meaning to Psalm 118:24: "This is the day that the Lord hath made; let us rejoice and be glad in it!"

I was thinking what a great testimony to the Lord they were, when another voice joined the choir. *So, other folk are up and about,* I mused. Though this voice was the only one I could hear, it must obviously be talking to someone. As I lay on my dorm bunk bed, I listened and wondered who the owner of such a thunderous voice might be. It was clear that she wasn't shouting...she was just loud.

My curiosity got the better of me, and by 5:20 I was down in the dining room drinking coffee with Susan Ledford, the owner of the voice. It only took me another five minutes to realize that I had met someone with a personality to match her voice: larger than life. I sat and listened spellbound to this interesting character until she stood up at 6:30 a.m. to "holler" a song upstairs at any of the remaining missionaries who still dared to be sleeping:

"When the red, red, robin comes bob, bob bobbing
Along, along
There'll be no more sobbin' when he starts throbbin'
his old sweet song
Wake up, wake up, you sleepy heads;
Get up, get up, get out of bed;
Cheer up, cheer up the sun is red
Live, laugh, love and be happy..."

This turned out to be a daily ritual; a new song each day, performed fortissimo and relentlessly until all errant folk were in the dining room waiting to say grace before breakfast.

After breakfast, we were invited to the Sunday service held in the small chapel above the garage and enjoyed familiarizing ourselves with the new culture while getting used to the intense heat with no air conditioning. The day was spent primarily enjoying the Lord and the people He was bringing into our lives, which allowed us to prepare for our mission work and the tasks we were to start in the morning. We were treated to lunch at the local beachfront restaurant, and then later we piled into a battered land cruiser for a short tour of the neighborhood.

There was a mixture of homes surrounding the mission. Some, though I would have considered them basic, were nicely appointed and of moderate size, boasting the amenities of glass windows, electricity, and water. Some others were small, box-like structures with fabric or wood shutters covering the windows. Most of these humble dwellings had no electricity or fresh running water. We drove towards the area where Iglesia De Dios is located, the church where our Vacation Bible Study was to be held the following day. The further away from the mission we drove, the greater the deterioration of the homes.

The poor living conditions did nothing to dampen the friendly smiles and waves sent in our direction as we drove by. However, by the time we reached Pastor Jaime's church, I was beginning to feel queasiness in my stomach and a restriction in my chest...I couldn't figure out why.

Back at Mission Del Mar we organized the supplies we needed to take in the morning and rehearsed the skits, songs, and "Panda" Bible study program we were intending to follow. We ate a delicious and hearty evening meal and enjoyed more fellowship before heading for our cold showers and bunk beds.

Monday again dawned with a chorus of a thousand birds waking up in the trees surrounding the mission. With the *best* coffee made available to us from 5 a.m., we had plenty of quiet time before our daily wake-up song and call down to breakfast. After praying, eating, and celebrating the communal devotional, we gathered the provisions we would need for the day and headed off to the church in the van, leaving the balance of our team to set up their service station and tools in the three-car garage of the Mission house. We were all to meet up for lunch at the church at noon.

Our plan was to have four-to-seven year-olds come to the morning session, and then repeat the same program for the eight-to-twelve year-olds in the afternoon after they had returned from school. It turned out that *God's* plan was for us to have a mixture of children ages eighteen months to sixteen years for whatever program they could make.

Our plan had been to use a local bilingual, middle-aged lady to be our interpreter. *God's* plan was for us to use two phenomenal young men, Josue (twelve) and Israel (nineteen), to be our interpreters. I shudder to think what we would have done without them!

Our plan had been to teach the children five or six Spanish Christian songs we'd been given and had practiced back in Florida. *God's* plan was to bring us Lisa and her entire local preschool and kindergarten class to teach us *their* songs and games. We had been told that the greatest asset a missionary can have is flexibility. I was beginning to understand why.

Iglesia De Dios is a cement block building approximately fifty by eighty feet in size, built by previous missionaries on the corner lot next to Pastor Jaime's home. It has windows set high and barred shut to prevent burglaries, and a metal roof with no cross ventilation. During July in North Honduras, this building made the most effective Turkish bath of all time. By noon and the end of our morning VBS, we were all dripping and exhausted. I was too tired to eat the sandwiches from the cooler, so I grabbed two bottles of water and headed for a wooden bench to nap. Since it was too hot for them inside, the men from the mission arrived and set chairs up in the shade out in the roadway to eat their lunch. One by one, the valiant VBS-ers recovered and joined them outside with stories of how our carefully made plans had been altered to fit His.

We loved describing the precious little children that the Lord had brought to us that morning. I will never ever forget eighteen-month-old Maria who arrived on the church doorstep by herself in a shabby cotton shift with tangled hair and dirty bare feet. As I gathered her into my arms and welcomed her to

VBS, I experienced the same feelings of unease and the chest constriction I'd suffered the day before.

Some of the men from the mechanic's program had planned to spend time in the afternoon putting together plastic bags filled with 2 lbs. each of rice, beans, and palm oil to take on a food drive in the evening. The VBS-ers, including myself, were invited to go on this mission with them. But first, I needed to muster the strength to head back into the sauna for a second VBS with a new class of children.

Again, God's plan differed from ours. Not only did we have new children of all ages, but we noticed many of the morning's class surreptitiously filtering back through the doorway as well. Halfway through our songs of praise, I spotted little Maria sitting on a bench at the back. As before, she had arrived barefoot and seemingly without any adult supervision. She wasn't, however, the only baby in our midst. Many of the ten- to sixteen-year-olds, boys and girls, carried babies on their hips. Since the daily task of the older children was to look after their baby siblings, we knew that these children would not be able to attend our VBS without them.

Maria was only one of many who didn't have shoes. It was the luckier children who sported cheap plastic flip-flops or dusty sandals. One of the highlights of the class was snack time, but I couldn't help wondering if the snack didn't end up being their main meal of the day, a thought that created more stomach unease and chest constriction.

It's not too much to say that by 4 p.m. we were exhausted, sweaty wrecks. The cold shower awaiting us at Mission Del Mar was pure joy, and it rapidly refreshed and invigorated our weary bodies. Thus, all six VBS-ers were ready to join the mission mechanics and go back into the evening heat in the open land rover to visit the remote areas of El Porvenir to deliver food. I had no clue what I was in for!

It took us over thirty minutes to reach the specific area that had been chosen for that day. It wasn't that it was any great distance. In fact, the area was probably only around five or six miles from the Mission. Rather, it was the rocky tracks that we had to negotiate that made any speed over ten miles per hour impossible.

The little cement block homes surrounding Iglesia De Dios started to look like mansions in contrast to the shack homes surrounded by barbed wire that we now encountered. Thin, joyless children stood silent and solemn in doorways or out in their barren yards, too discouraged to give the smiles and waves we had experienced closer to town. Their tattered clothes did nothing to cover their cuts, scratches and bruises— tokens won from the unforgiving environment that they lived in. Their bare feet were encrusted not only with dirt, but with dried blood from wounds suffered on rocks and barbed wire encountered throughout their day. There didn't seem to be a mother who wasn't supporting a baby on her hip.

"Where are the fathers?" my soul cried out. Perhaps in their small fishing boats far out in the Gulf of Mexico; or slaving in the pineapple fields for mere pennies per hour; or maybe standing on a street corner drinking or gambling away the few dollars earned—a futile effort to relieve the pain of knowing they could not provide for their families.

Plastic milk and soda bottles were precious commodities. Lined up against the sides of the shacks, they were used to

THERE IS NOTHING LIKE LOOKING INTO THE FACE OF ABJECT POVERTY TO CHANGE ONE'S OUTLOOK ON LIFE.

collect whatever water was available from the rivulets close by – water that was reliant on the rainfall over the mountains just a few miles inland. The bulk of this water, however, was often contaminated either by human waste on its journey to the sea or made briny from the salt brought by the tide's backflow.

We visited as many shack homes as we had bags of food... perhaps fifteen to twenty...clearly fewer than were needed! We prayed over each home and the family that lived in it while the neighbors looked on, hoping that their home would be next and that the supplies wouldn't run out before we reached them. The unease in my stomach grew close to nausea and I had to keep reminding myself to breathe through my constricted lungs. There is nothing like looking into the face of abject poverty to change one's outlook on life.

I don't think a word was spoken on the way back to the Mission. We were well into our meal before we managed to regain our lighthearted spirits. Sharing is the greatest way to put your thoughts and emotions into perspective. Slowly and without needing to be encouraged, we each disappeared to write our day's experiences in our journals.

Excerpt from my journal: Monday, 4 July 2011...

Today I was given the greatest gift I have ever been given: a glance into our world with a little of God's perspective! Today is indeed Independence Day...independence from worldly values...and given a total dependence on God's values. Life is not all about what God can do for me. Life is all about what I can do for God.

As I lay in my bunk that night, I became aware that the uneasiness in my stomach had departed, as had the tightness in my chest. God had made His point, and I had seen it clearly! I was rewarded with a feeling of peace that is with me to this day.

Vicki's plaque had attained a new and profound meaning. Having been given a little of God's perspective on His world, I knew that I had to change my way of life and the reason I was living it. I had no doubt whatsoever that I was being called to serve in missions and that I wanted to devote the rest of my life to that end. I had no way of knowing, however, what that might "look like," and I would have to wait on the Lord to show me.

When I was asked to give a presentation to my church soon after our return to Tampa, I wondered how I could convey the impact our mission trip had made on me. I picked up a copy of the application form that I had completed back in September and saw a great opportunity to re-answer those important questions for the Cypress Point Congregation.

Application Questions and Answers:

Have you had any previous experience as a missionary?
"Yes"

If so, what was your overall impression of the experience?
"It was life changing"

Do you have any experience in teaching?
"Yes – I discovered you learn far more than your pupils do!"

What talents or craft skills do you feel you possess?
"A little of God's perspective!"

Why do you want to go on this trip?
"To be given the opportunity to find out what it is that I can do for God."

What do you hope to gain/achieve by going on this trip?
"A little more of God's perspective!"

How do you think this trip might change your life?
"In any and every way possible, but hopefully to make me a better servant to God."

Perhaps the best-known missionary is Paul of Tarsus, who wrote so much of the New Testament in the Bible. Having come to know Christ on the road to Damascus, he converted to Christianity and devoted the rest of his life to serving God through His son Jesus Christ. His missionary journeys led him from Jerusalem, around most of the Middle East, north to the Black Sea and as far west as Rome. Maybe not remarkable in this day and age, but when understanding that most of his mission journeys were done on foot or in modest boats, it gives us a different perspective. Through his many letters to the new church he helped establish throughout the known world, he teaches us to focus on what it is that is important to God; how we should follow the teaching of Jesus in order to be who it is that God wants us to be. From his words, we learn an important truth: contrary to what the world is constantly telling us, life is not about us!

"This is how one should regard us: as servants of Christ and stewards of the mysteries of God."
1 Corinthians 4:1 (ESV)

Gary and Peggy Williams

CHAPTER 4: PORTRAIT OF A WALK IN FAITH

"Faith is the strength by which a shattered world shall emerge into the light." {Helen Keller}

I FIRST MET Peggy Williams and her husband Gary in 2011 at Mission Del Mar, during a church service held in the chapel above the garage. Gary served as pastor to the little congregation of English-speaking missionaries and faithful from the surrounding community.

I enjoyed the service, but at the time I was more involved with getting to know my own mission companions than I was with getting to know or building a relationship with either Peggy or Gary. It wasn't until subsequent visits that I had the opportunity to sit down and get to know them. As they shared their tale, I realized I was listening to one of the most extraordinary stories I have ever heard.

Gary Williams was born in Aberdeen, Mississippi. He was the third child in a family of ten children – five girls and five boys born to his mother within a fifteen year period. He remembers most of his early childhood as being part of a busy, noisy family in which each sibling had to fight for attention. His happy existence ended abruptly at the age of ten, when it was discovered that his young mother had two types of cancer. A valiant two-year fight ensued, full of pain and experimental procedures. Then at age thirty-six, his mother died, leaving an impossible task for his grieving single father.

His seven younger siblings were placed in an orphanage; his baby brother was adopted, and Gary "escaped" to Panama City Beach. There, at the age of twelve, he lived on the streets and had to fend for himself. It took but a short time for him to discover a windowless cement-block hut at the rear of a vacant property, a hut much like the many basic structures he was to encounter later in life. It was this simple hut that he made his home for the next five years.

 Gary's infrequent visits to his father and siblings in Mississippi did little to keep his heart firmly connected with them. In later years, once he was older and more mobile, he managed to visit them more often in an attempt to bond with the family. It was on one of these trips home that Gary first met Peggy in a local bar, where she was celebrating her graduation from high school.

Peggy Harlow was born in 1950 in an old house in the middle of a cotton field in Nettleton, Mississippi. She was the first of two children, both born at home and without professional help. Her brother arrived five years after her. She remembers her childhood as a huge struggle because of their poverty and the constant relocations needed as her father, a farmer, tried to find work. It was her father who insisted on taking his family to the local Baptist church, and Peggy grew to love every minute spent within its walls. She also loved going to the Pentecostal Church with her aunt when she visited.

When she was eight years old, Peggy became a born-again Christian and gave her life to Christ at Vacation Bible School. One year later her world came crashing down when her parents divorced. Her dad left them for another woman, and Peggy's mother gave up on God, gave up on life, and sank into a life-threatening depression that left her unable to look after or support her children. Nine-year-old Peggy stepped in to take care of her brother, who was so much younger. She had to tend to a sick mother, cook, clean, and run the house while still going to school. Their grandparents managed to provide some meager support, supplying them with essential food and clothing.

It took a full two years before Peggy's mother recovered enough to get a job. But life didn't change very much for Peggy. She was still left to cook, clean, and run the household, but now each morning she would get up at 4 a.m., prepare breakfast, and pack lunch for her mother. After this she would feed herself and her brother before getting them both off to school. In the afternoon she would arrive home and have dinner ready for the family by the time her mother returned from work. It was through her diligence in making sure both her brother and she did their homework that both children excelled at school.

Sometimes her aunt still invited Peggy to her own Pentecostal church, but Peggy was never able to attend the little Baptist Church she loved. God was not mentioned at home anymore since her mother still continued to hate life and all men with whom she came in contact; and it was for this reason that, as a teenager, Peggy was never allowed to date or do anything that most young girls enjoyed.

After graduation and with no great plans for what she wanted to do with her life, Peggy threw herself into celebrating her new status by going to a local bar with a friend. That was the night she met Gary.

Their attraction was immediate, but as Gary still spent most of his life in Florida many miles to the east, their relationship proved difficult. Gary's father, however, happened to be a friend of Peggy's family. Once he heard about their chance meeting, he began to play Cupid, acting as an intermediary and giving each of them updates on how the other was getting along. His patience and encouragement paid off. Gary moved back to Mississippi to get a job and live with his brother. Peggy and Gary fell in love and married while they were both still teenagers – Gary was nineteen and Peggy just eighteen.

Six months after their wedding Gary was drafted into the army, and then, having finished his six-month military train-ing, he joined his peers when they were sent to Vietnam. He and Peggy had barely been married a year when he left, and their infant daughter, Pamela, was just one month old.

Like a great number of other servicemen who participated in the Vietnam War, Gary returned home a very different person. Peggy was bewildered by the change in him, not know-ing how to handle his mood swings and his constant need to "get away." He was heavily into drugs and alcohol, blaming his addiction on the solitary life he had led while abroad, the chal-lenging experiences of war, and his need to numb his mind with the oblivion that the drugs provided.

Peggy battled on without being able to tell anyone of the pain and emotional abuse she experienced at home, as she feared that Gary would lose his rank and position in the army if she sought help. Peggy continued in misery, until a transfer to Germany in 1975 brought hope that the situation would change. While there she conceived their second daughter almost immediately, and Melinda was born in January, 1976. Gary was still unable to shake his addictions and still continued his "single" lifestyle, leaving his family alone while he went on his constant binges.

Eventually Gary decided a separation would be best, telling his wife that he needed to sort out his addiction problems by himself. Devastated, Peggy returned to her home in Mississippi where she was served with divorce papers just a few weeks later. It wasn't until this point that Peggy realized there had been another woman, a soldier, involved all along. Gary entered a second marriage just a few days after the divorce was finalized.

Peggy fell into a depression that is typical of many folk who have experienced such a betrayal, and she felt the same emotions that must have plagued her mother so many years before. She started the life of a single mom with her little girls, building a hatred and resentment of men. As retaliation, and in an effort to re-establish her self-image and confidence, she hit the party and bar scene; flirting, teasing, and taunting any attractive men in the vicinity, then dropping them like hot bricks once they showed a serious interest.

IT WAS THE GRIM, LAUGHING VOICE OF THE
DEVIL, TELLING HIM THAT HE (THE DEVIL)
HAD WON, AND GARY WAS NOT GOING TO
RE-AWAKEN FROM HIS STUPOR.

It was a man from her workplace who eventually managed to crack the shell and penetrate Peggy's fortress of resentment. William Dwayne had received similar treatment from his first spouse. He was a divorcee who not only understood and listened to Peggy's painful journey, but showed empathy, patience, and love. In May of 1979, Peggy succumbed to William's charm and agreed to marry him. And thus, she unwittingly jumped headlong into another dysfunctional union. The marriage, however, lasted seven years. This time when the decision came to part ways, it was a huge relief, and she bounced back into her life, content and grateful to be single.

In the meantime Gary had divorced his second wife and returned to the United States to continue a wild single life complete with long hair, a beard, and a Harley Davidson. He contacted Peggy, who was understandably reluctant to meet at first but eventually agreed to let him see his daughters after the four-year absence from their lives. His lifestyle hadn't changed, and although encouraged by Peggy, his visits were infrequent and seemed awkward.

It was in Verona, Mississippi, a year later that the inevitable happened. After a week-long binge of drinking and drugs, Gary suffered an overdose. He recalls little of the time leading up to his near death experience, but distinctly remembers a voice speaking to him as he fell through the front door of his home. It was the grim, laughing voice of the devil, telling him that at last he (the devil) had won, and that Gary was not going to re-awaken from his stupor once his head hit the floor.

Not fully knowing what he was doing, Gary fell towards the couch, but instead of reaching the horizontal position he had originally wanted, he collapsed with his one arm hooked around the end of the furniture. This managed to prop him into a slouched kneeling position, his head held above the floor. Even in his semi-conscious state Gary knew he mustn't give in to his overwhelming desire to lay his head down.

He desperately needed help. Fading in and out of his drugged stupor, he stared at his phone where it sat taunting him on the side table, just out of reach. He floundered around with his free left hand and felt the cord. Mustering his strength, he gave it a yank in his direction. The phone crashed to the floor just in front of his knees. But whom could he call?

Inexplicably and out of the blue, Wayne Wyatt's name and number came to mind. Wayne had been a good friend to both Peggy and Gary while they had lived in Germany many years back. Wayne had needed Gary's help to pay for an air ticket back home from Germany. Gary had given him some money, and Wayne had promised to reciprocate whenever Gary needed help in the future. This had happened so many years previously that it was nothing short of a miracle that Gary remembered both Wayne's words and his telephone number in his drugged condition.

Gary punched in the numbers, not knowing if his efforts to hit the keys were coming anywhere near their target. Then, un-doubtedly another miracle, Wayne answered the phone! He told Gary not to move an inch and then rapidly drove one hundred miles to pick up his friend. Wayne and his wife Debbie lifted Gary into his truck and took him home to keep him alive and to help him revive and recuperate.

Since the time that they were together in Germany, Wayne had become a born again Christian and a pastor. He tended to Gary with unconditional love, asking nothing other than for Gary to promise to come to church with him at least once before leaving. In one of his weakened moments Gary made the promise, though secretly he had hoped to avoid the issue during the two months it took him to recover.

One Thursday morning when he felt strong enough, Gary decided to get on his Harley and ride off to continue his former lifestyle. Perceptive enough to anticipate Gary's plans, Wayne confronted Gary with the fact that he couldn't leave until he had visited the church. They argued for hours, but eventually it was agreed that Gary would go to the church that evening as long as Wayne agreed to ride on his bike with him. By the time they arrived, the visiting evangelist was well into his program, and Gary slipped into a seat as far back and out of sight as possible. No sooner had he sat down, than the preacher stopped his program and asked the late arrival to come forward. He had a message for him.

A very hesitant Gary walked to the front and the evangelist proceeded to talk to him about his life, using details that no one other than Gary could have known. He finished by adding that the Lord God wanted to start a relationship with him. At this point in his life Gary truly didn't believe there was a God. Yet he knew that something very strange was going on. It was a much-shaken Gary who returned to his seat at the back of the church. Once there he sat down with his hands resting on his knees, palms up, and prayed, "God if you do exist, I need to feel you."

As the evangelist continued his talk, a door at the rear of the church opened, and a man walked across the sanctuary and down the center aisle. He continued to the pew where Gary sat, bent down and placed his hands into Gary's. Gary finds it hard to adequately describe this experience and the feelings of peace, joy, and comfort that spread through him as they touched. He has no doubt that it was Jesus who placed very real, human hands into his own that day.

Gary didn't leave that Thursday, but continued his walk with Jesus while staying many more months with his friend Wayne in Moundville. From the moment he accepted Christ as his savior, his life did a complete "180." He went straight out to look for a job, and found one immediately in a boatyard that had proclaimed there were no jobs available. He worked hard and loyally, being promoted from deckhand to boat mechanic within six months and reaching his goal of Riverboat Pilot within five years, a feat that would normally have taken eight or nine years.

Eventually, Gary made a commitment to visit his daughters and to mend the damaged relationship with both of them. He finally made peace with Peggy, who was at first both skeptical and wary of his motives. After many, many months of wooing her and trying to prove the sincerity of his changed lifestyle, Gary managed to persuade Peggy that he truly still loved her and that with God and His Son Jesus as the most important part of their relationship, their re-marriage would work. On January 23, 1988, Gary and Peggy remarried, twenty years after they had first said "I do" as teenagers.

They set up their home near Wayne Wyatt and the church in Moundville, Alabama, and enjoyed the comfortable lifestyle that their (now) lucrative careers provided. They studied the Bible and grew in knowledge of the scriptures; they started a group of wandering gospel singers that traveled the southern states and evangelized in churches wherever and whenever they were invited. Gary, who had only been able to take his GED in the army, was called to preach the Gospel.

Six years after their wedding, Wayne once again became instrumental in their lives. He asked Peggy to join their church team on a mission trip to Mexico, knowing that Gary had planned to go to a bike rally in Sturgis, South Dakota at that time. Though irritated at not being able to do what he wanted, Gary decided to join the mission team. This trip marked a monumental change in the direction of their lives.

Suddenly mission work became their focus. Their professions enabled them to earn more than enough money to make several mission trips a year to Mexico. They packed their car with food, clothing, and provisions and hit the road to various missions where they assisted in every practical way to serve God's poor. Spreading the gospel and building more churches and mission houses became their life.

It was on one such trip, while driving along the main thoroughfare through a remote region in Mexico, that Gary heard a voice telling him to take the next road on the right. He did, but the road continued to stretch for quite a long way, becoming increasingly narrow and bumpy. When the road narrowed to little more than a track, Peggy and their travel companion, Ms. Kendall, asked Gary where they were going. He told them that he had no idea, but that God had told him to turn and he was going to continue until the Lord told him to stop. He got the instruction to stop when they reached the village of Santa Isabelle. They stopped, introduced themselves to the few people they met, and promptly held a church service under a large shade tree by the roadway.

Santa Isabelle proved to be sparsely inhabited, its simple huts spread over a large area. They befriended the pastor of a small local church, and they were able to distribute some Spanish Bibles and other supplies needed by this impoverished congregation. They left the village to return to Alabama, feeling a deep love for the little community they'd just visited. By the time they got home to Moundville, Gary had been inspired to go back to Santa Isabelle to build a larger church and start a mission.

Three weeks later, in obedience to God's request, Gary and Peggy quit the comfortable income and positions that they had held for twelve years and headed to Santa Isabelle with a truck load of their possessions.

It was their own home church, as well as other churches that they had befriended on their gospel singing tours over the years, together with Wayne and their families, who supported this new ministry. They began the task of building a church and a small home for themselves on the outskirts of Santa Isabelle, and Walking by Faith Ministry was born.

The mission and church grew over the next ten years, and by the time the Williams were given God's marching orders to Honduras, their Mexican mission was well-equipped and run by a cluster of God's faith-filled missionaries. God brought Gary and Peggy to La Ceiba in 2009, where they found some beautiful beachfront property just to the west of the town; it is here that they started a new Walk by Faith, and it is here that they lived at the time I met them.

Each day of their lives is a challenge. Each day brings more work, more joy, and more of God's people to help. Each day is a new opportunity to spread God's Word and the Good News of the Gospel. Each day is another reason to walk by Faith in the knowledge and certainty that God will provide. What a joy it is for me to be able to share their incredible story!

"He who dwells in the shelter of the Most High will abide in the shadow of the Almighty."
Psalm 91:1 (ESV)

Renea Phillibant Harris

Chapter 5: Reflections from a Nurse

"You cannot connect the dots looking forward; you can only connect them looking backwards. So you have to trust that the dots will somehow connect in your future. You have to trust in something, your gut, destiny, life, karma, whatever. This approach has never let me down, and it has made all the difference in my life." {Steve Jobs}

PERHAPS ONE OF the most rewarding side benefits of spending time as a missionary is the opportunity to meet so many wonderful people. With some, this opportunity develops into the privilege of building a relationship and discovering a life-long friend; the type of friend that you later thank God for giving you as a treasured gift. Renea Harris is one such gift.

Renea (Phillibant) was born in 1952 in Mt. Clemens, Michigan, the sixth of seven children. Her early life was lived outside the Christian faith, but a near-death motorcycle accident that her father experienced in 1962 resulted in a three-month hospital stay that changed the direction of both his and his family's path. Coming close to death must always be a "wake-up" call. Renea's father gave up his heavy drinking, and the trauma of the accident helped him to focus on what is important and to give his life to Christ. Three years later he was to die of colon cancer.

Renea met her husband David at a wedding when she was just seventeen years old, still in high school. She and David dated for three years before marrying on May 11th, 1973. After completing high school, Renea pursued her dream of going to nursing college, graduating in 1976. She threw herself into her career for seventeen years before receiving the call to join a mission trip.

Many of us wonder what skills and talents we might possess that can serve God on missions, and Renea was no exception. She considered herself "just a nurse"! To you and me, that is a substantial skill set, and one I would definitely enjoy having–but Renea was reticent to believe that her workday expertise could actually be of use to the Lord. Despite this, she signed on for a medical mission trip to Haiti. It changed her life.

I'll let her share the experience in her own words:

"While I was there, a woman came in with her 2-year-old daughter. The little girl was dying of AIDS. She weighed just 10lbs, and all I could feel were bones. She had a vacant, empty look in her face, and the look of despair in her mother's eyes was haunting.

That night I went to sleep thinking about this baby. I woke up several times throughout the night hearing the words, 'Ye who have so little faith trust in me and doors will open'. The words continuously played in my mind all night long. I was so tired and pretty fed up, but then I remembered I had been the one who had been afraid that I wouldn't recognize when the Lord would send me a message; so He spoke to me *all night* long, just to be sure I heard him. The Lord does have a sense of humor!

That next morning I got up and actually felt energized. There was a pay phone across the street from the hotel and I called my husband to tell him of my experience and that I felt the Lord was calling me into full time ministry. Being the wonderful man he is, David said that he would support me in whatever decision I made. This is a phone call I don't think he has ever forgotten, as at that time I was earning 60% of our household income, and this change would become just as big of a sacrifice on his part, as it was on mine.

It wasn't until after I had made the decision that I questioned myself, saying, *'What on earth am I doing?'*"

This is when Proverbs 3:5-6 started to become such a real part of Renea's life, and what she would cling to so many times in her future. Renea's story continues:

"I must share that when I went from the corporate world and into a life of working for the Lord, I secretly thought I would be leaving all of my troubles behind.

Let me tell you, I couldn't have been more wrong. For you see Satan was just waiting to pounce on me.

Having given a four-week notice to my employer, who thought I was crazy, I immediately began to volunteer with Missionary Ventures International.

Two weeks later my aunt died, making it necessary to take time off to bring her to Michigan where she was to be buried. Then eight weeks later, while I was in Africa, my mother died. Her death was obviously a tragic part of my life; however, I must also tell you this was a true answer to prayer. I had been silently praying for years that I would never have to see my mother lying in a casket.

Satan might have believed that he was going to win and get me away from missions, but you see I considered the timing as being a blessing. My grief was real, but God knows our every need and our every thought. Philippians 4:6 states that we should tell God what we need. Even silent prayers are heard. God knew I would be in Africa long before I knew I would be there, and He chose that time to take her home.

The third attack took the form of an itchy rash all over my body that persisted for seven months after returning from Africa.

The fourth attack was severe altitude sickness while in Peru at 15,000-foot elevation. After this Satan must have given up on me, as I went nearly two years without another major attack.

I FELT PERHAPS, AFTER ALL, I MUST NOT HAVE THE RIGHT QUALIFICATIONS.

On June 4, 2003, I left on another two-week medical mission trip to Ghana with ten others. There were seven adults and three teenagers. The teenagers in the team acted more like adults than the adults did! The older members of the team were defiant, argumentative, and complained about everything from our living conditions to the meals being served. The teens never complained about anything. My only comfort as I went to bed every night was reading 2 Corinthians, 1:3-7, the Bible chapter on the Lord God of Comfort.

I was so devastated by the trip that I went directly to the office at Missionary Ventures on my return in order to talk with the leadership. Opening my heart, I told them how I felt I was a total failure at leading this team and maybe this was God's way of telling me that I didn't belong in missions anymore. I felt that perhaps, after all, I must not have the right qualifications.

What I was told in response was both motivating and comforting - none of us are qualified, but if God is calling you He will give you what you need to meet His calling. Back to Proverbs 3: 5-6!"

Less than three weeks after returning from Africa, Renea left for Nicaragua. She had just got home and truly wanted to go to Michigan for the CMA Rally, and desperately needed a break. "God, don't you know I need rest?" she cried. God's timing for the most part is not our own. She reluctantly went to Nicaragua and very rapidly learned why she needed to be there.

"After church on Sunday we took the team to visit a re-nutrition center. This is a home where babies and children that are malnourished are brought in from the community and surrounding mountain area. I was immediately drawn to a 17-month old girl named Lillian. She had been at the home for close to two and a half weeks. Her weight was 13.42lbs when she arrived and she now weighed 14.08lbs; just a little over a half-pound weight gain. She was sitting in an infant seat, as she had not learned yet to walk. Her eyes had that same empty look in them as the baby in Haiti.

I held her for close to two hours, talking to her and taking her outside in an effort to stimulate. She just sat without any display of emotion until I turned on the viewfinder on my camera. She watched, mesmerized, as I went from one picture to another. She began aimlessly to reach for the camera, although she still remained expressionless. When it was time for lunch, one of the workers handed me her bowl of rice cereal and she sat straight up on my lap and leaned forward, opening her mouth like a bird with each spoonful.

We went back to the center a week later and as I picked her up she immediately reached for my camera and was eagerly touching the button that would change the pictures from one to the next. It was an obvious leap in a direction to physical and mental health that was both a shock and a joy to my system.

As we were leaving for the second clinic day we were told that the pastor's wife, Azuzana, who was usually the one doing the evangelism, was now not able to be with us as her daughter was ill... so, the question was asked, who is going to do the evangelism? Even though ours was a medical team, our primary purpose of going was to help the local pastors grow their congregations in order to reach people for the Lord; not just to meet their physical needs. In other words, the medical clinic is a vehicle to draw people into the church. It was the words from Isaiah 6:8 that sprung into my mind, *"Then I heard the Lord asking, "Whom should I send as a messenger to my people? Who will go for us?" And I said, "Lord I'll go! Send me."*

I found myself with my hand raised up in the air offering to do it. Then the fright set in—what did you just do, Renea? I had been the one who needed guidance from my pastor's wife when I had first started in missions in order to get over my fear of praying out loud with groups. I was simply terrified!

The first group that came to me was a family of five. We were standing outside by the side of the building. When we finished praying I looked up and we were surrounded by thirty people. These people were hungry to hear God's word and to learn how to receive Jesus as their personal savior. I quickly realized it hadn't been me talking; yes it was my voice, but the words had come from the Holy Spirit.

Soon after this I had the joy of introducing a boy name Miguel to Jesus. He had never heard the name of Jesus and had never in his life seen a Bible. I was able to spend quite a bit of time with him, and our eyes seemed just glued to each other, making us totally unaware of the others around us. He listened and asked questions. When we were through I asked him if he would like to receive Jesus as his personal Savior and he said yes; so we prayed together."

When I joined Renea on a mission trip to El Porvenir in July 2011, she was already a ten-year missionary veteran. Her passion for missions, her organizational skills, her medical background and her love of God's people were obvious skills and talents that the Lord was using through her willingness to serve – a true one of His PIGS! I will be forever grateful to Renea for her willingness to use these wonderful gifts to lead our mission teams around the world, and for changing my destiny by introducing me to the wonderful world of missions.

"Trust in the Lord with all your heart, and do not lean on your own understanding. In all your ways acknowledge Him, and He will make your paths straight." Proverbs 3:5-6 (ESV)

CHAPTER 6: PARABLE OF A TEA ROOM

"What would you attempt to do if you knew you could not fail?"
{Robert Schuller}

AT THE END of 2004 my associate and colleague Teresa Rogers from First in Real Estate, where I was managing broker, came to live with me while she transitioned from one house to another. During the six months that Teresa shared my home, we formed a close friendship; the type of friendship that is built on a trust that only God can instill. We did many things together while never encroaching on each other's privacy or independence. We would walk most mornings, and drive together to Baylife Church in Brandon on Sunday and to Bible Study Fellowship on Monday evening.

On a Sunday in February 2005, while returning from church, both Teresa and I had an idea—the same idea. Our brainstorm started with my irritated observation that I would have to return to Brandon the following day for a Bible since Lifeway Bookstore was closed on Sundays and New Tampa, where we lived, was devoid of any bookstore, let alone a Christian one. Teresa added her equally irritated comment that New Tampa pretty much lacked anything particularly cultural, creative, or interesting. As we turned onto Morris Bridge Road from I-75, a plan was born. We both visualized a cute little English tea room located somewhere in New Tampa and rolled into one with an Old Curiosity Shop and Christian bookstore. The detailed vision came with a name: Miracles.

LOOKING BACK ON THOSE DAYS, IT IS EASY TO RECOGNIZE GOD'S TOTAL CONTROL OVER EVERYTHING THAT HAPPENED IN OUR LIVES.

Our excitement grew. Neither of us had any doubt our inspiration was from God, and it had come with the instructions merely to obey and to try to accomplish the dream. It did seem bizarre that we were being asked to start three businesses in which neither of us had any experience: restaurant catering, retail sales, and a bookstore. However, we had total trust and faith that God knew what He was doing in making the request.

Teresa was sitting at an open house in Lutz the following Wednesday, and by the time she came home the complete, detailed business plan was finished—all sixty-some pages of it! Her outline was wonderful and, as Teresa is the first to admit, her inspiration was a complete gift from the Lord.

Neither Teresa nor I could sleep or relax for the next few weeks as God had us busy honing the details, finding possible locations, checking leases, outlining physical requirements, and determining licenses needed. Our biggest task was working out how we were going to finance the enterprise. All this was happening at the same time we ran our real estate businesses, Teresa was buying and moving into a new home, and I was finishing and publishing *The Power of Present Day Parables*. Looking back on those days, it is easy to recognize God's total control over everything that happened in our lives.

Our BSF (Bible Study Fellowship) study that year was on Genesis, the first book of the Bible, and a book that excited and interested us both. We reached chapter 26, which describes Isaac's stay in Gerar, the land of the Philistines where his father Abraham had lived many years before. Isaac had planted crops that "reaped a hundredfold," and the Bible tells us that he had become so wealthy that the Philistines envied him and he was asked to move on. Thus, Isaac had relocated his considerably large household some miles away to the Valley of Gerar.

Here he proceeded to dig and re-open his father Abraham's wells that had been closed by the Philistines over the years. As he opened each well and found fresh water, the herdsmen of Gerar would argue with Isaac's own herdsmen about the ownership of the well and water. Wisely, Isaac did not contend the issue; he would just move on to digging another well until he eventually dug a well that didn't cause a dispute or argument. Isaac knew it was at the well that didn't create a problem that the Lord would bless and help his household flourish.

What an incredible lesson Teresa and I learned. Our prayers immediately became focused on needing the Lord to open and reveal the wells He wanted us to use. We prayed over decisions with regard to location, leases, web design, décor, construction work, licensing, financing, and left the "well" solutions for the Lord to provide. Our prayers were answered on a daily basis as God opened all the doors He wanted us to go through and closed all the ones He wanted us to avoid. "Miracles" was the perfect name for our establishment, as small miracles occurred every day to fulfill God's plan and purpose.

We found a brand new 1600 sq. ft. bay in a business park within walking distance of my home, and both Teresa and I knew immediately that this was to be the location for Miracles Tea Room. The accommodating landlord agreed to the long list of changes and additions we would need. Our wish list included upgraded ceilings and new lighting, additional parking and a fenced exterior patio at the rear; a cobblestone courtyard at the front and a boarded attic space for storage. Our restaurant licensing required changes that involved plumbing and electric for a commercial kitchen, tiled floors in the tea room area, an additional bathroom, and an office and storage space that housed a floor sink in the closet as well. My wonderful son-in-law, Pickles, took over the tasks of constructing the large U-shaped registry area that was to house the two large metal trees that became a signature of the establishment and a fabulous means for displaying merchandize. He hung and installed all the kitchen cabinets. In fact, Pickles became our official handyman and was one of the essential components throughout our enterprise.

In May I took Teresa to England for a ten-day trip to experience the "real" English tea room atmosphere. For the most part we stayed with my dearest friend Maggie Monk and her family in Chesham, and then travelled with Maggie to stay in Wells and Kingsbridge at properties the Monks owned in the magnificent English countryside of Shropshire and Devon. This gave us the opportunity to tour a variety of tea rooms at hand. Just as important, it was here that Teresa got to know the incredible Maggie, about whom I had been talking for so long. I had known Maggie since 1965 when we auditioned in the West End of London and got parts in the chorus of *Hello Dolly* with Mary Martin.

Maggie had been diagnosed with Lou Gehrig's disease early in 2002, and the horrendous symptoms were truly taking their toll on her life. Her faith and incredible bravery made a huge impression on Teresa, and it was she who suggested we add Maggie's name to the title of our tea room as we travelled back on the plane to Tampa.

In June of 2005, four months after our initial idea sprang to mind, Teresa organized a trip to Dallas to the huge Retail Mart where retailers order their wholesale products. Frankly, though knowing merchants must get their supplies from somewhere, I hadn't realized places like this existed. That trip became one of the highlights of my life. The mart was a huge shopper's paradise. Until then, shopping had not interested me in the slightest, but Teresa's expertise, organization, and astute perception were amazing. They triggered in me a love and interest that was to carry me over the next five years.

Together we toured the enormous buildings stacked with dozens of levels and filled with hundreds of booths. Though totally exhausted by the end of the three-day trip, we were both elated with what we had bought and the relationships we had established with the wholesalers. These relationships remained firm and trusted over the entire lifetime of Miracles. Our time together in Dallas is something locked in my heart to be treasured forever.

The period between July and November became a blur of busy-ness. Like most everyone else who is starting a business, we looked to the banks in order to get our financing; only to find that, if the business hadn't been in existence for three years, hadn't shown a profit or owned its own property, then it was not going to be financed by them!

It was at this time that Teresa and I made the biggest leap of faith in our lives. Teresa was in her fifties, recently divorced and totally on her own. I had my two daughters and one family close by, but was self-supporting and in my sixties. When my step-son Roland heard of our enterprise, he made his point with this question: "Mom, are you sure you want to do this at this time in your life?" Although I jokingly replied, "I'm really not sure. Perhaps I should wait until I'm eighty," I was well aware of the jeopardy I was putting myself in for my future.

Neither Teresa nor I took the decision lightly, but after much prayer and guidance from the Lord, we decided to raise the $100,000 each, the seed money that was needed, by taking out second mortgages on our homes. Real estate was close to being at its all-time high, and getting the necessary appraised value was not an issue.

We looked at the work of three or four artists before choosing Pam Parrish at Leopard Tree Design to paint the mural and walls of the tea room. Her brilliance at capturing the essence of the British countryside from our photos and her talent at using walls as her canvas was an integral part of what Miracles became.

We were also really pleased with Ron Hine, who introduced us to ComCash for our point of sale system, a system that seemed to cover every need in tracking the three businesses we were running under the same roof. Our website designer Jim Ekstrand not only produced an incredible website, but also supplied gorgeous framed photographs to decorate our walls and to sell; Jim came with the added joy and benefit of being the husband of our dear friend Avril, our long-time colleague from First in Real Estate.

We were introduced to Mary Iorio, who in turn introduced us to our other "Miracle Workers": Tina Wilkins, our food and beverage manager, and Carole Stevens and Christine Freeze. Teresa's friend Annette Baker had a sixteen-year-old daughter, Alyse, who wanted to join us as well. These ladies became life-time friends and the most valuable gift of our entire Miracles experience.

The licensing with Hotels and Restaurants was a challenge, but bit by bit and one by one, all the obstacles were addressed and solved. The build-out was completed, the phone and cables connected, and we initiated the advertising on the new event to "happen" in New Tampa. Everyone who came through the front doors of Miracles was handed a Bible and a marker, and asked to write their favorite verse on the cement floor before the carpet was installed. Many of these folk already had their verse memorized, but many had never opened a Bible and had to search for a passage on the spot! It became a source of joy to all "Miracle Workers" to know that each one of our customers, colleagues, friends, and business associates would be standing on God's word.

MANY CHOICES AND DIRECTIONS WERE PUT ASIDE, YET GOD SHOWED HIS FAITHFULNESS BY OPENING HIS BOUNTIFUL WELLS ON EVERY COURSE THAT WAS NEEDED.

Wisely, Teresa had arranged for our inventory from the Dallas Mart to be delivered over a staggered period. Boxes upon boxes started to arrive, and Mary, Teresa, and I, while still learning the system, started to get the contents recorded into the new POS (Point of Sale) system. Our staff had grown to six or seven and we manned the shop on a schedule that we thought might work. Remaining flexible was a vital attribute and a great lesson to learn for my future walk with God.

Once the carpet was installed, Tina and Carole joined us as we started to put Miracles together! Both Teresa and Carole's interior decorating skills came into full bloom, and Carole's experience and talent as a window dresser for Macy's became an invaluable ingredient for our success.

Tina worked on our menu, keeping it simple enough to manage but interesting enough to gain a satisfied clientele for the tea room. Mary, Tina, Teresa, and I went to class and took the necessary exam to become licensed food preparers. Then we visited and chose Sam's Club for our fresh produce and US Foods as our wholesale food distributers.

No decision was made without prayer. Many choices and directions were put aside, yet God showed His faithfulness by opening His bountiful wells on every course that was needed. By the beginning of November, Miracles was ready, and it had become evident that, with God's grace, our Miracle Workers, together with Teresa and me, had created something very special for New Tampa. By now we could look back on many wells dug since we started our journey, so many that God blessed as we used them, but many that were unproductive and had to be left unused.

On November 8, we were ready to throw the first of four or five trial parties to fine-tune our skills and launch us into the world of retail and catering. We opened the doors to our first customers: a party for Avril, who brought seven or eight of her friends.

On November 25, 2005, to our great delight and my eternal gratitude, Judith Law flew her sister over from England. Judith had brought my dearest friend Maggie to me, enabling her to celebrate the opening of Miracles and Maggie's Tea Room. Maggie died in Chesham, England on March 2, 2006; her 60th birthday.

"Then they dug another well and they quarreled over that also, so he called its name Sitnah. And he moved from there and dug another well, and they did not quarrel over it. So he called its name Rehohboth, saying, 'for now the Lord has made room for us, and we shall be fruitful in the land." Genesis 26:21-22 (ESV)

CHAPTER 7: PARABLE OF A PARTNERSHIP

"For it is mutual trust, even more than mutual interest that holds human associations together." {H.L. Mencken}

FOR MANY YEARS I wondered why it was so important to be "equally yoked" with a spouse. After all, as long as you chose a "good" person, were personally strong and in control of your own thoughts and convictions about Christianity, as long as you trusted God with your life...what could go wrong? Ultimately it wasn't marriage that taught me the reasons why being evenly yoked is essential; it was another type of partnership, my partnership with Teresa Rogers.

Teresa and I had opened a tea room in November of 2005, and as Miracles and Maggie's Tea Room progressed into its first year, it became very apparent to both Teresa and me that at least one of us needed to be working in our new business enterprise in a fulltime capacity. This had never been our plan, since both of us were making good incomes as real estate agents. Although Teresa was newer to the real estate business, she had great local knowledge, keen business acumen, and a wonderful work ethic. I had been an agent for 25 years and a broker since 1983. Leaving our jobs was not an easy decision since neither of us had expertise in any of the three businesses—bookstore, restaurant catering, and retail—that

Miracles encompassed. Teresa voted me into the role of owner/manager purely because…I spoke with an English accent!

Knowing that the business couldn't afford to pay me close to what I had been getting in real estate, we began to pray for a solution. Eventually Teresa came up with a plan that seemed acceptable. We would start a real estate partnership: The Miracle Team of First in Real Estate. Instead of my working in real estate, I would refer all my real estate business and clientele to Teresa. This meant that she would have to spend all of her time and focus in real estate, trusting me with the day-to-day running and decisions needed at Miracles. The real estate partnership would pay me a percentage of its income in order to subsidize the meager income I was to get from Miracles.

So it was that in August of 2006 I threw myself into my new mission: the full-time position of managing and running Miracles and Maggie's Tea Room. This entailed food shopping, inventory, scheduling, promotion, networking, advertising, and serving customers. Teresa and I would still make all financial and policy decisions together. The timing seemed perfect as Mary, our store manager, had decided to move back to Melbourne with her family. It was also at this time that God brought us Kristen Heath, a friend of my daughter Vicki's and a phenomenal cook, who fit right into our family of Miracle Workers. Carole Stephens, having been a window dresser at Macy's for many years, had an incredible talent for décor, and she took over the huge responsibility of our interior decorating, which changed constantly with each and every season.

News of our good reputation, excellent food and quaint originality spread throughout the Tampa Bay area; though we were not breaking even yet, the considerable Christmas retail business was more than encouraging. We forged into 2007 knowing that the New Year was to be a banner year, for a variety of reasons. We were becoming better known. I recognized many areas where we could economize without jeopardizing quality or value. I grew wiser with purchasing inventory and utilized better hours with a more efficient staff scheduling. On top of this, the seemingly great economy had brought us lots of happy customers willing to spend. At the end of the year we showed a gross income increase of 35% and a net increase of nearly 41%.

NOTHING CAN PUT STRESS ON ANY
PARTNERSHIP SO MUCH AS A
FINANCIAL CHALLENGE.

We were close to breaking even for the year. It certainly looked as though the trust Teresa had placed in me was paying dividends. Having discussed our figures, we agreed that I could increase my salary from Miracles in order to relieve some of the subsidizing pressure placed on the real estate end of the Miracles Team. The real estate market was just beginning to feel a down turn, and the volume of referrals I was able to give Teresa was dwindling as I had been out of real estate for more than a year. We decided to consolidate some high-interest debt we had incurred on the water softening system and other equipment by getting a small credit line from the bank. Thus, going into 2008, we seemed to be in "good shape".

January and February were on par with the prior year, but then came March. It felt as if everyone had left the planet! We didn't need to look at the figures to know something was devastatingly wrong. By the end of April we knew we were in an untenable situation.

Nothing can put stress on any partnership so much as a financial challenge. Sickness usually draws people together. Though a life that is threatened by illness or death is devastating to everyone involved, the gravity of the situation immediately puts things into perspective and rapidly brings the realization that nothing is as important as the life and health of a family member or partner. Financial stress, however, usually brings guilt, blame, distrust, arguments, and desperation.

I will never forget the dinner meeting Teresa and I had at her home at the end of April. We needed to discuss options, ideas, plans and a very uncertain future. Teresa was tremendously challenged by the most horrendous real estate market of her lifetime. Four out of five contracts, even if she managed to get a home under contract, would fall apart. Housing values were crashing. Buyers sometimes had to wait six to twelve months before they were able to close on a short-sale purchase; many would walk away from their transaction thinking they could get an even better deal with another home that had now come on the market. Large debt loomed heavily over her head with sparse likelihood of her being able to get out from under it. Now, with little control or time for involvement, Teresa was under the dark cloud of a floundering business that was sucking funds from an already empty bank account.

My situation was just as grim. At the age of 61, I had given up a lucrative career that I had held for over twenty five years. I had leased my home (where I now owed far more than it was worth), and rented a one bedroom apartment in an effort to reduce my expenses. At *Miracles* I worked close to seventy hours a week, trying to justify the less than meager income it was giving me, and trying every conceivable angle to make more money. I was also concerned that Teresa might want us to "abandon ship", even though we still had two and half years to go on our lease.

Having worked in the tea room for many months, I could tell that the take out and catering side of the business provided a better return because it took fewer man hours and made a better profit. Our group tea parties were also money makers,

I BEGAN TO UNDERSTAND THE TRUE
MEANING OF BEING EVENLY YOKED.
IF BOTH PEOPLE IN A PARTNERSHIP HAVE
TOTAL FAITH AND TRUST IN GOD, AND BOTH
SINCERELY GO TO GOD WITH OPEN HEARTS
AND MINDS FOR THEIR GUIDANCE,
A PARTNERSHIP CANNOT FAIL.

but the set-up of the tearoom was not conducive to private parties as long as I had to cater to other walk-in customers.

The retail side took up precious space while at the same time delivering a static investment in the depressed economy of the time. I wanted Teresa to see the wisdom of re-designing the space and putting our efforts into those two avenues. It was going to take trust on her part. She truly didn't like the idea of take-out catering, loved the present design and décor, and was concerned, among other things, that the alterations might not look good and would cost too much. But instead of our sinking into the "stress trap", it was at this meeting that Teresa said something very profound.

"Jackie, the Lord has laid it on my heart that I truly don't have to trust in you...I have to have trust in HIM. We need to focus on doing the next right thing." This one insight allowed us to release our own fears and doubts and to focus on what needed to be done, and that would be, as Teresa put it, "the next right thing!" We prayed together, and were confident that whatever decisions we made were coming from Him. No matter the outcome, as long as we tried to do the right thing, He would have us covered. I felt that Miracles had been a "call" from the outset, and as such was more of a mission than a big business enterprise, and quite definitely something that we needed God to control.

We decided that a visit to the landlord with our Profit & Loss statement in hand, a frank account of exactly where we stood financially, would enable him to make an intelligent decision on how best to handle the fact that we were not going to be able to pay the full rent. Thus we made it the responsibility of the landlord to guide our next steps. He could close us down and re-rent the space (unlikely in the current economy), and perhaps sue us for the remainder of the lease payments, or he could help us limp through the present situation.

As I lay in bed that night, thinking over Teresa's faith-filled words, I began to understand the true meaning of being evenly yoked. If both people in a partnership have total faith and trust in God, and both sincerely go to God with open hearts and minds for their guidance, a partnership cannot fail. God is always good, always faithful, and is totally in control. It is *His* plan, for His purpose, and He has all the answers that are needed. He is able to change any heart; change any circumstance; and is certainly able to bring two opposite opinions in line with each other. However, if either person in a partnership does not have the faith to trust in God for their guidance, the equation is most often doomed to fail.

So many parallel lessons in faith can be gleaned from the Bible, which after all is the book that teaches us what true faith is. But a favorite of mine is the walk of faith that Ruth takes together with her mother-in-law Naomi. Naomi had left Bethlehem in Israel with her husband and two sons in a time of famine, and had settled in the land of the Moabites. Both her sons had married Moabite women. Her husband and both sons died while there and Naomi decided to return to Bethlehem, the land of her birth. She tried to persuade both of her daughters-in-law to return to their families and stay in Moab. Orpah decided to take Naomi's advice, but Ruth was resolute that the "next right thing" would be to stay with Naomi, to look after her, and make sure she returned home safely. It was then that she uttered those amazing words of faith, "For where you go, I will go, and where you lodge, I will lodge. Your people shall be my people and your God my God."[1]

She stepped out in faith and into an unspoken partnership with her mother-in-law. She was doing the next right thing, knowing that The Lord God of Israel would protect them, no matter what circumstance they found themselves in.

The two women reached Bethlehem, and though Naomi sank into depression, Ruth continued to care for her, working hard in the fields day after day, gathering the grain that they needed to survive. Boaz, a kinsman of Naomi's and a wealthy landowner in Bethlehem, saw Ruth out in his fields and through others learned of her faith and servant's heart. The couple met, fell in love, and married. But the greatest reward the Lord bestowed on Ruth was the result of their union: a son, Obed. Obed was to become King David's grandfather and a direct ancestor of Jesus. Quite a legacy!

Neither Teresa nor I knew what the Lord's plan was for Miracles and Maggie's Tea Room, but we had no doubt that our job was merely to step out in faith, trusting God, day after day, doing the next right thing. It turns out a tea room was truly an excellent school and testing ground for becoming a missionary.

"Trust in Him at all times, you people; pour out your hearts to Him, for God is our refuge." Psalm 62:8 (NIV)

"Do not be unequally yoked with unbelievers. For what partnership has righteousness with lawlessness? Or what fellowship has light with darkness"? 2 Corinthians 6:14 (ESV)

---

[1] Ruth 1:16

CHAPTER 8: PARABLE OF THE HUMMINGBIRD

"You talk to God, your religious.
God talks to you you're psychotic." {Doris Egan}

AS A MISSIONARY, one of the questions I most frequently hear is, "How do you know that the Lord is *calling* you to *go?*"

It's a great question! But it is one that, as far as I am concerned, has many answers; the call has come in different ways for different missions, tasks, or trips. Having not become a Christian until very late in my life, it took many years of reading the Word, participating in Bible studies, listening to messages at church and simply walking in new life before I was totally comfortable with giving up control and letting God handle everything the way *He* wanted. My daily prayer had become, and still is, "Lord, please open all the doors you want me to pass through today, and close all the ones you don't." It never ceases to amaze me, however, that He does exactly that!

Everyone's communication with the Lord can be different, but the one thing that seems to be consistent with us all is that the Lord confirms His message over and over again. My first mission call was a distinct voice, during a service, telling me to sign up to go on the trip organized by my church. I obeyed, but much against my will...it was definitely NOT what I personally wanted to do, or had any previous need, call or dream of doing. In other words it was *not* on my "bucket list"! Having obeyed by signing up anyway, God then orchestrated my life in such a way that all my objections and reasons for not going were taken away. I was left with little option than to go.

The second time was a totally different proposition. I had already received the call while in Honduras through a distinct physical tightness in my chest, a feeling of unease, sorrow and hopelessness that wouldn't abate until the decision in my heart to be "open" to the Lord's missionary instructions brought me peace. I knew without a shadow of doubt that the Lord was about to change my life forever, but I had no idea how. I just needed to wait; and this time the wait was a very short one.

My daughter Vicki had picked me up from the airport in Tampa late on Saturday night, and on the drive home I was able to share with her my knowledge that the Lord was calling me to Honduras in some capacity. She was totally understanding and supportive, to the point that she promised to introduce me to her good friend, Doug Torres, one of the owners of A Cup of Organic (organic coffee from Honduras) who was, she thought, from Honduras himself. Doug had invited Vicki to his home on the following Tuesday for lunch and I was now invited to go along. While with this dynamic man of God, and as we ate a traditional Honduran lunch that he had personally made for us, Doug told us about The City of Hope Orphanage – a home for abused, abandoned and neglected children that his brother Juan Carlos had been involved with for some time. Juan also sat on the board of directors after it had been established by his great friend and mentor, Pastor Jose Inestroza. Doug excitedly showed us video and photographs of the orphanage, and the lovely children being nurtured there.

Though feeling an affinity with City of Hope, I could not see how I could be of help, as I didn't speak Spanish and didn't feel I had any skills to offer them that would help. Doug excitedly told us of Pastor Jose's visit that week, and that he knew that both his brother Juan Carlos and Pastor Jose would love to meet with us. Vicki immediately invited all three men to join us for lunch at her home on the following Friday.

Lunch on Friday was a delight. Meeting both Pastor Juan Carlos and Pastor Jose was a joy and a privilege. I was told of how the home was established ten years before, why it had been needed, as well as much of its history. Pastor Jose told of his ultimate dream and goal, to eventually add two more homes to his list: a safe haven for the elderly, and a home for abused women and their children.

City of Hope was presently being run by a wonderful angel of mercy, Alicia Smith, who had come to them five years previously from California. Alicia was of Hispanic background, spoke fluent Spanish, and though she had never felt a deep love for children prior to her "call" to help the orphanage, she had all the gifts, skills and talents that God needed to change the lives of His suffering children. Many of the children had entered the orphanage as babies and toddlers, taken off the streets of Tegucigalpa and the surrounding area by the equivalent of Child Services. Now, ten years later, most of these children were in an age group ranging from ten to eighteen, though there were two or three that were younger, having arrived later to City of Hope.

Pastor Jose explained through our interpreter Juan Carlos that the children's needs had changed dramatically. As babies and toddlers the needs were more basic; a loving environment that included clothing, food and a roof over their heads. By the time Alicia had joined the equation a new building with a living room, two bathrooms, and two large side by side dormitories (one for the girls and one for the boys) had been built. This allowed the converted chicken coup that they had all originally lived in to be used just for laundry, sewing and crafts, kitchen, and dining room. The new building, though only six years old, was showing signs of shifting down the precarious slope of the mountainside, resulting in a huge crack in the entrance wall and a sinking living room floor.

So now there was a new and urgent need...a new dormitory, not only to relieve the overstressed present building but in order to separate the girls from the boys, now mostly teenagers. Pastor Jose's demeanor had changed from just telling a story to anguish about a problem for which he could see no answer. Juan Carlos repeated the need, not losing any of the urgency or anxiety in the translation. It didn't take special discernment to recognize the problem; twelve boys and eleven girls, mostly now in their teens, living in one building in side-by-side dormitories and sharing bathrooms that were only partly functional.

ALTHOUGH I HAD NO IDEA HOW I MIGHT HELP,
I WAS BEING CALLED BY THE LORD TO OBEY.
I JUST NEEDED "TO GO", AND THE LORD
WOULD HANDLE THE REST OF THE DETAILS!

It was Pastor Jose's plea, "Please, please come to City of Hope to see for yourself...can you do anything, anything at all to help?", that captured my heart. Although I had no idea how I might help, I was being called by the Lord to obey. I just needed "to go", and the Lord would handle the rest of the details!

Juan Carlos started to check the cost of flights over to Honduras, in order to get an idea of what the monetary commitment might be. Pastor Jose was due to fly back to Honduras the following week, and Juan Carlos had a three week business trip to Honduras organized for the beginning of September; could I join them for that third week when Juan Carlos could once again act as an interpreter? Flights into San Pedro Sula were $100 less than flying into Tegucigalpa, and though a four-hour car trip away, it was decided to fly me into the less expensive airport. My flight was booked then and there, over lunch on my very first meeting with Pastor Jose, and amazingly, within a week of my returning from my first mission trip.

I was invited to visit Pastor Juan's church, Grace Outreach, the following Sunday, as Pastor Jose was to give his testimony to the small congregation and it would give me another opportunity to learn more about this remarkable man, and the City of Hope that God had led him to establish back in 1999. The bi-lingual service was wonderful, as was the food, fellowship, and joy shared at the meal following.

Both of my daughters, Vicki in Tampa and Abi in Houston, could not have been more supportive of their mother making another trip back to Honduras so soon, and did everything to encourage me to do what it was that God wanted me to do to help City of Hope. None of us knew exactly what this help might be, but all of us had no doubt He would reveal it in His time, and to His purpose. We all knew that nurturing children was not one of my greatest gifts, so we felt that most probably my involvement would be angled more in the promotion and speaking field. But I wanted a sign and confirmation from the Lord that this was in fact what He wanted, and that helping in some capacity at City of Hope was what He had in His plan for me. My daily prayer for God to "open and close doors" for me became more and more relevant and important, as I totally relied on His guidance for my life by being my "Doorkeeper".

At the end of August and beginning of September that year, the west and central regions of Texas were experiencing some of the worst fires in recent history, with smoke blowing all the way across the state. The hummingbirds that usually inhabited the north-western regions of the state were being "pushed" over to the Houston area, and at my bidding (because hummingbirds are my favorite bird), Abi went out and bought a couple of hummingbird feeders to welcome the tiny refugees.

As I sat at the airport in Miami awaiting my flight to San Pedro Sula, Abi sent me a picture and text message showing that the hummingbirds had arrived, and she promised to look after them in my absence.

I was met at San Pedro Airport by Pastor Jose and Pastor Juan Carlos. They brought Alicia with them for me to meet and get to know a little better on the long drive south to Tegucigalpa. Being tired from the flight, I was content to listen to the conversation more than participate, and to enjoy the gorgeous scenery as we headed south. I was able to get to know more of the children, the City of Hope, its history, its particular challenges and Alicia's role since taking over the running and administration for the previous five years. Though showing nothing but love and enthusiasm for her job, it didn't take a great deal of perception to recognize the weariness and toll that the five years of 24/7 responsibility and physical effort had taken on this small dynamic lady.

Not speaking Spanish and not having any experience with the very individual Hispanic Honduran culture made me realize that, although I might have been able to get over my limitations in the nurturing children field, I could do little to help in the everyday running of the orphanage. I have to admit that my prayer at this point was that it wouldn't be *this* door that the Lord would open and push me through!

It was dark by the time we arrived in Tegucigalpa, as we made a detour and dropped Juan Carlos off with some of his relatives in Comayagua. We did some grocery shopping, and got home to Casa Hogar, "City of Hope", around 8 p.m. local time. It was 10 p.m. Tampa time; I had left home in the very early morning and was totally exhausted, so I expected to sleep well even though in an unfamiliar bed. Wrong!

While I lay comfortably in a bottom bunk with a cacophony of noises continuously attacking my undefended ears, I remembered the noises I had experienced in my first mission trip to El Porvenir and Mission Del Mar. These sounds were slightly different. We seemed to have a rivalry between the many local roosters, hundreds of dogs, and a couple of donkeys in the surrounding homesteads. No one was going to be defeated, no one had any idea of, or respect for, the time of night, and no one was about to give in! The din continued all night, through to dawn, and up until 5:30 a.m. when the voices of the children joined the chorus.

Boiling water in a mug in the tiny microwave took four full minutes, but the resulting cup of tea was a blessing. I hugged it and went out onto the patio of the mission house to sit and watch the activities below as the children did their chores, had their breakfast and got ready for school while I read my devotion for the day. Though I knew that there must be some adult direction at the children's dormitory, all the chores and activities seemed to be done without any instructions or direct supervision. It was a hive of activity as children swept, mopped, collected and carried washing, cleaned their teeth, dressed in their uniforms and collected backpacks ready for school.

After assembling for communal prayer on the concrete pad outside their dorm, the younger children left the compound first, dressed in navy blue trousers or skirts with crisp white shirts or blouses. I was later to discover that they had a good mile to mile-and-a-half walk to their elementary school along the very rough local track; downhill for most of the way to and uphill for most of the way back. The middle school children left about fifteen minutes later, dressed in white shirts and beige trousers, to go to their school that was just a five-minute walk away. I ventured down the hill to the kitchen and dining room after the children left to meet up with Alicia (Ali) at a time I hoped would not interfere with the everyday schedule of events.

Ali was waiting and ready to take me on a tour of the City of Hope. The property seemed to be about three acres in size, but it was very difficult to assess, as the dimensions were in no way uniform. There was a fence surrounding the property, but none of the sides were straight, continued in any specific direction, or bore any resemblance to what I had experienced as a "parcel of land" in the past. I actually had the opportunity to measure the perimeter of the fence at a later stage, together with my always-willing helper Bayron, and made a pretty accurate scale drawing, but as there was no guarantee that the fence was built on the actual property line to start with, there is still no way of assessing the true dimensions.

There were three buildings. The kitchen and dining room where we started the tour were part of the first (and once the only) building of the orphanage, and had originally been a 90' x 20' hen house. It consisted of three rooms: the laundry room at the north end, a sewing/craft room in the middle, and the kitchen/dining area at the south end. It was the south end of this structure that illustrated the basic problems shared by all the buildings. It showed huge cracks, slippage, and foundation damage. One of the faithful mission teams that came to serve the orphanage had recently "under-pinned" the building on the southeast end to arrest more damage.

The second, newer building was the children's present dormitory and, although only five to six years old, it had a truly massive crack around the front entrance showing a fatal flaw in the construction. The main living room had a visual and decisive dip in the middle. Its shifting foundation had managed to compromise the already stressed plumbing pipes to the point that some of the toilets and showers were blocked, either from the natural need of constant maintenance due to the huge volume of waste water that is the result of so many people using the facility, or from the more likely and obvious shifting movement of soil.

The third building, built at the same time as the current dorm, was the two story mission house. The ground floor had two bedrooms with an integral bathroom, an eat-in kitchen and a large living room/dining room. The second floor had four bedrooms with two integral bathrooms. Each room had two bunk beds, bringing sleeping capacity up to four missionaries in each. Theoretically this enabled mission teams of up to sixteen, but an extra couple of folding beds and some air mattresses in the large living room had permitted teams of up to twenty in the past. There was a small but efficient kitchenette that enabled folk to keep themselves in snacks and drinks in between meals while visiting. The structural problems with this building were not so evident, but there had been some major water leakage into the back wall of both bedrooms on the ground floor that had only recently been repaired, and the flashing around the bottom of the upper balcony was in need of repair.

Having asked Ali what I might do to help her while there, I returned upstairs to the mission house in order to tidy and sort out the book case and craft area that the last young mission team of students had left in disarray and that Ali needed sorting out. As with any tidying process, the initial step is to pull everything out, off shelves, and planted in the middle of the floor. I did this with my usual gusto, but it wasn't until I had cleaned and polished the shelves and was returning the books, boxes and other items back that I came across a beautiful jigsaw – a picture of a lovely hummingbird! Being an avid jigsaw puzzler, I couldn't wait to start on it, but put myself on the task at hand before succumbing to the temptation.

It actually took me the rest of the day to re-organize and finish tidying the shelves and the plastic containers, and I started to make mental notes about how to help the general challenge of un-housed "stuff" in the room like the pillows, sheets, towels, and pillowcases wrapped in large plastic bags and heaped against the end wall. I took a break at lunchtime to spend time getting to know some of the children. They were only too happy to get to know me, and the language barrier became evident but not insurmountable as they were only too willing to await my Spanish/English dictionary-assisted communication attempts.

I then started a second tour of the property, being led by my new little friends who were eager to show me their treasures and the important stuff in their lives. I will never forget Jonathan as he proudly took me to see his possessions, all neatly lined up on his top bunk; that, and the plastic container at the end of the bed were the only things he seemed to be able to call his very own.

HE WAS ASKING ME TO USE THE TALENTS,
ABILITIES, CONNECTIONS AND EXPERIENCES
HE HAD ALREADY GIVEN ME
OVER PAST YEARS.

Though not having much in comparison to what my own grandchildren had, there did not seem to be a "lack" of anything that is truly important. They seemed way more (dare I say) 'happy', and certainly more disciplined, organized, and willing to help than any large group of children I had experienced before. The fact that each one had their own chores that they completed without direction or complaint was amazing; the fact that each one thanked God on their own, before each meal, and then took good care of each other's needs was refreshing; the fact that they all joined together to worship and learn about the Lord each evening before going to bed and each morning before going to school was enlightening.

I was later to learn from Ali of the challenges, sorrow, and hardship that she had to endure in the teaching process and that it had taken many months and years of adversity, loneliness and prayer for her to succeed in changing the untrusting, ragged street urchins into the loving children of God that they were now. I could tell that the strength and diligence it had required of her had taken its toll, and I feared that Ali was close to being burned out.

I returned to finish my own chores in the mission house living room, so that I would be able to reward myself with starting the 500 piece jigsaw later in the evening. As I worked I prayed. I prayed for Ali; I prayed for the children; I prayed for Pastor Jose and the need for a new dorm that had become more and more evident with each passing hour. I prayed for the Lord to show me in what way it was that He wanted me to help. After supper I joined Ali and the children for their Bible study and then headed back up the hill to my jigsaw puzzle.

Over the next few days, just like the hummingbird puzzle that was coming together piece by piece, my instructions from the Lord came together to build a picture of exactly what He wanted me to do for City of Hope. He was asking me to use the talents, abilities, connections and experiences He had already given me over past years.

It became apparent that in order for people to be able to respond to the needs at City of Hope, it was necessary, first of all, for people to know who they were. In today's world that equated to a website! A place that described in words and pictures "Who We Are", with a description of how they had grown to be the precious place they had become; "Our Mission Statement", an account of what they were ultimately trying to accomplish; "What Our Goal Is", in order to illustrate what their immediate need was (that of building a new dormitory); and finally to provide a practical way in which folk could easily and safely make their donation through PayPal and become personally involved.

It would be necessary to communicate the call for help to everyone; the mission teams who presently visited and helped the orphanage; new teams willing to answer the call to come and help physically with the construction; folk who were able to help through donations; and then finally the folk who would be willing to offer time and talents to raise funds in their own ways and in their own communities for this need that was presented to them. I knew nothing about construction, but the first step, communication and promotion, was something of which I did have knowledge. Something that the Lord had given me the time, talent, and experience to learn while running a real estate business for thirty years and having owned a tea room, book and gift store for the past five.

Ali included me in her trips into town to go to the market, the grocery store, and to visit their local friends and prayer partners for prayer meetings and Bible studies. Though not able to communicate in Spanish, I was received with enough love, joy, thanks and gratitude to last a lifetime. The open way in which I was accepted and encouraged to stay was lovingly expressed by Ali and everyone else I came into contact with, and especially the children. I grew more and more comfortable with the environment, and I had even begun to sleep through the noise at night with aid of some ear plugs I had found. As the hummingbird jigsaw progressed, so did the picture full of ideas and instructions from the Lord as to how I could help City of Hope and its quest for a new dormitory.

Juan Carlos was not going to be able to meet up with us again personally during my week-long stay, as he had to return to the coffee plantations in the northern regions of Honduras; but he promised to meet up with me soon after my return to Tampa. He had asked Ali to drive Pastor Jose and me out to visit his family on the southern side of Tegucigalpa in a suburb called Tatumbla. We drove out to have lunch with them that

Friday, and I had the chance to meet Juan and Doug's wonderful mother and their sister, who spoke fluent English.

As I finished the jigsaw puzzle I realized how well the colors matched the curtains in the living room of the mission house upstairs, and I wanted to be able to somehow stick the pieces to some type of foundation in order to make it a picture for the wall, knowing that it was significant and one of the signs that the Lord had given me to tell me that it was here at Casa Hogar, City of Hope, that I was meant to be. Something told me to look behind the bookshelf that I had just tidied – I did, and there it was, a perfect square piece of hardboard exactly four inches wider and four inches longer than the finished puzzle, allowing an exact two inch border all around to be its frame. Some might say this was just another coincidence, but I know better! I mixed some of the water color paints that were a part of the craft sets on the bookshelf to make a perfectly matching deep mauve two inch border, and then used the craft glue to stick each piece into place on the hardboard backing.

The jigsaw was complete and ready to be hung – the perfect picture for the room it adorned, and a constant reminder of God's faithful messages and confirmations. I knew without a shadow of doubt that the Lord needed me to return to the orphanage sometime early in the next year and that I was to be instrumental in starting the construction of the new dormitory, though I had no clue as to how. I was already committed to a second mission trip to El Porvenir with my church on March 17-24, and flying down to Tegucigalpa on the 24th seemed good timing to save on additional flight expenses. Both Alicia and Pastor Jose agreed, and seemed excited that I had made the decision to return to them. Having learned of my former career as a dancer, Pastor Jose asked me to consider choreographing a dance for the girls to perform at his church at Easter.

As I flew back to Tampa, excited about telling my family about my new "career" direction from the Lord, feelings of peace and joy engulfed me to the point that it drew tears to my eyes, a peace and joy that stays with me to this day.

Juan Carlos called me soon after his return and I agreed to attend his church service the next Sunday. He wanted to speak to me and to officially introduce me to his congregation and have me tell them about my trip and the Lord's calling. I was delighted to share my love, feelings and ideas for City of Hope, and humbled by Juan Carlos as he gave me a pin to wear with a map of Honduras, and a blessing for the work that the Lord was about to use me for. As we sat eating the delicious meal Doug's wife had prepared for us all, Juan shared his deep concern for City of Hope and its future, as Alicia had shared with him and Pastor Jose her feelings of exhaustion and the need to ask them to look for a replacement for her. She had given them approximately a year to find someone suitable. Though I had understood that Ali was truly suffering fatigue, it had never crossed my mind that she was considering an end to her mission.

Both Juan Carlos and I knew that my call from the Lord was to help with the effort to get a new dormitory built, and the necessary promotion and advertising it would require. I could do little but promise to keep this new situation in my prayers. It was over this Sunday lunch of fellowship at Grace Outreach that Juan Carlos told me that both he and Pastor Jose had discussed what my exact role should be, and that the title of

Missionary Field Coordinator would cover the type of services I was hoping to provide both in the States and in Honduras.

As it had not truly been in my heart to make a career of catering, it was with some relief that I handed over Miracles Catering to Ghada, who owned the Dash of Salt N Pepper catering business, and let her take over my commercial kitchen area in Cory Lake Isles. She joined my Business Networking International chapter as their caterer, and I converted my seat in the chapter to that of Missionary. I concentrated my efforts in getting the website up and running, having the necessary videos presentations put together, business cards made, and generally spreading the news of my new mission in life throughout my large network of friends and business colleagues.

The next five months flew by, as I knew they would, and true to His word, the Lord continued to open the doors He wanted me to go through, while closing those that He didn't. There was never a day that He forgot to let me know that I was doing exactly what He was asking me to, confirming in only ways that He could orchestrate His instruction to follow this path to City of Hope.

"For I know the plans I have for you, declares the Lord, plans for welfare and not for evil, to give you a future and a hope. Then you will call upon me and come and pray to me, and I will hear you. You will seek me and find me, when you seek me with all your heart." Jeremiah 29: 11-13 (NIV)

CHAPTER 9: PARABLE OF A PERFECT PLAN

"All human plans are subject to ruthless revision by nature, fate, or whatever one prefers to call the powers behind the universe." {Arthur C Clarke}

PRIOR TO BECOMING a Christian, I had spent my adult life like many others, adamantly believing that if there was a God...*doubtful*...he would never micromanage or even want to organize the mess we were all in down here on earth. I could see very little purpose or plan for my existence or, for the most part, for those around me. I was disappointed in much that had happened in the past, and worried about what the future seemed to promise. Most of the fun and delight I did feel came from family relationships and the beauty of the world around me, both of which I felt to be a "freak of nature." One exception was ballet. Dancing skillfully to beautiful music gave me joy and provided my reason for living; in retrospect, it replaced the need for God – my plan was to be a professional dancer, and it didn't seem necessary to involve God in my pursuit of that dream.

Before becoming a Christian in 1993, the thought of relinquishing control of my life to God was very foreign to me; I didn't know Him and I didn't trust Him. The idea of allowing anyone to be my "Doorkeeper", to be in charge of and lead me through my life, day by day, was so remote that it wasn't even an option to consider. Why would God even *want* to control my day, let alone bother to have a plan for it?

THE PROBLEM WAS CONSTANTLY FORGETTING HE *WAS* IN CHARGE, BECAUSE I'D TRY TO TAKE BACK CONTROL MERELY THROUGH HABIT.

But then He orchestrated my coming to know Him in a miraculous way, intricately weaving my own and other people's lives to converge at one small point in time in order to make His presence known to little old, insignificant "me". It was a pivotal event creating more than a paradigm shift; my beliefs and way of thinking turned a full 180 degrees. Further doubt of His desire to be a part of my life and His ability to micromanage anything He chose was no longer an issue. There seemed little other option than to dive into Christianity with my usual enthusiasm!

However, it took many years of practice in "letting go and letting God" for me to become proficient in actually doing so. At first it seemed weird that when my plans had to be changed in favor of His, they ended up, without fail, so very much better than I could have imagined. Truly the best part of my new Christian role in life was the opportunity to put the Lord in charge of it, and to be honest it didn't seem that difficult for me to do this; the problem was constantly forgetting He *was* in charge, because I'd try to take back control merely through habit.

In recent years however, having made it my daily prayer for Him to take charge, I have become so comfortable with the arrangement that I dread to live my life in any other way. So it was that the call for me to go back to Honduras to work at trying to get the new dormitory constructed may have come as a surprise, but I never doubted it. Neither did I hesitate to set things in motion.

Like all other times the Lord had called me to His purpose, He started to confirm His call in many ways—some of them small nudges, some of them blatant statements. I started to see dreams and visions that included the children as they performed dances that I had choreographed for them. When I returned from my first visit to the City of Hope at the beginning of October, my beloved Community Bible Study class was mid-way into a study of the Book of Isaiah; it was no coincidence that we were delving into chapter 6 that particular Thursday, in which God asks, "Whom shall I send, and who shall go for us?" and Isaiah answers, "Here I am! Send me."[1]

The colleagues in my class were surprised but supportive when I shared my intention to go back to Honduras for a five or six month mission trip in March, and tears came to my eyes as the beautiful old missionary hymn "Here I am Lord" was the devotional worship song of choice that same day. The following Sunday the very same verses of Isaiah were used as the theme of Pastor Dean's message to our congregation at Cypress Point. And of course, the ancient hymn, that I don't remember ever hearing before, was played two or three times on Moody radio as I listened in my car.

Support and encouragement rolled in from all directions, and we started to compile the videos, photos, and information needed to build the new City of Hope website. There was a great deal of work, time, and some expense involved, but everything materialized and started to come together. By December we had a working model to show to Juan Carlos in

---

[1] Isaiah 6:1-13

order to get his advice, along with the necessary documentation for making the PayPal account a "Not for Profit" way for supporters to be able to give money and have their donations be tax deductible. By the end of the year the site was fully operational and I was able to contact all the past missionary team leaders to invite them to visit, and to become a part of what we were trying to accomplish by sending their photographs and videos of City of Hope to be added to the website.

Missionary teams from Michigan, New York, North Carolina, California, and Florida rallied together to start raising funds for the dormitory construction. The communication between all past and present missionaries and team leaders flowed freely with love, joy, and camaraderie in the sole aim of becoming a part of God's plan for their beloved children at Casa Hogar. Pastor Greg's Freemont Wesleyan Church put out a $10,000 challenge to be matched by them dollar for dollar. I organized a couple of fundraisers that were great fun: a wine tasting and silent auction at the end of November, and a High Tea in February, 2012.

By March 17th, the day we left for Honduras with the mission team from Cypress Point, we had over $22,000 in the new dorm construction fund. My first stop was El Porvenir, where we did a construction project and a women's conference. The week flew by, and it seemed no time at all before Renea and I flew down from San Pedro Sula to Tegucigalpa. Ali met us at the airport in the evening and we drove the twenty minutes to Casa Hogar, City of Hope.

As we traveled to Tegucigalpa, I had mentioned to Renea my concern after my trip to City of Hope the year before, that Ali was feeling "burned out". Ali met us at the airport, but the woman who met us was an invigorated lady, full of enthusiasm and energy—a drive that had not been at all apparent during my last visit, and I wondered what had made the difference. By the time we arrived at the orphanage we knew the reason, as Ali could not wait to let us know the incredible turn of events.

ALI HAD BATTLED IT ALL WITH ONLY
HER TRUST THAT SHE HAD BEEN CALLED
BY GOD TO RESPOND TO HIS NEED.

Her daughter Adriana and son-in-law Rick had visited Ali at City of Hope for the first time, just before Christmas. They had fallen in love with the children, and before they left to go back home to California they both had felt the call to come back to Honduras and serve at Casa Hogar. Ali was amazed... neither Rick nor Adriana had shown any previous interest in missions, let alone what they knew to be the great challenge of serving at Casa Hogar and the commitment that it required.

For the previous few years, Adriana and Rick had served as youth pastors at their church, His Light on a Hill, in California. When they returned to California in the New Year and told their church of the call to serve as missionaries, the church not only responded with encouragement and enthusiasm about the prospect, but stepped up to support them in their new mission field financially as well. Suddenly God's Plan was being revealed. All the trials, the desperate loneliness, and the huge challenges that Ali had endured over the past six years now made sense and had meaning. It was all a preparation for the time that her family would come over to Honduras to join the mission to serve the orphanage and to help her grow Godly children for Honduran society and culture; children who would otherwise have been left to suffer poverty and abuse in the streets. This wonderful and childless couple from California would now have twenty two children in their family, with the promise of many, many more once the new dormitory was built and the existing building repaired.

God had a wonderful plan, the Perfect Plan, from the very beginning...before Ali said yes to her call in 2006...before Pastor Jose was called to establish the orphanage in 1999. The grief from losing her husband, and the emotional pain as she fought through the ensuing loneliness; the unending challenges from the surrounding culture; the discipline needed to teach seemingly unresponsive children; the intimidating threats from unknown adversaries; Ali had battled it all with only her trust that she had been called by God to respond to His need.

The truth is that no one truly knows why he or she, in particular, is being called; merely that, like Isaiah, they are being told to obey. We are asked no more and no less than to trust God and *GO*, being confident that He has a plan, and that it is far more splendid than any plan we could conceive on our own.

"*Many are the plans in the mind of a man, but it is the purpose of the Lord that will stand.*" *Proverbs 19:21 (ESV)*

CHAPTER 10: PARABLE OF THE LOST WEDDING RING

"We think having faith is being convinced God exists in the same way we are convinced a chair exists. People who cannot be completely convinced of God's existence think faith impossible for them. Not so. People who doubt can have great faith because faith is something you do, not something you think. In fact, the greater your doubt, the more heroic your faith." {Preacher}

WHEN I EARNESTLY began reading the Bible in 1996, I started with Matthew, Mark, Luke, and John, the evangelists who give us "The Good News". Like many readers when first introduced to the Gospels, I began to relate to the twelve disciples who Jesus called to follow Him, since I recognized many of their character traits in myself. There are two disciples, however, with whom I found myself particularly affiliated.

One, Peter, was immediate and obvious to me since I am a hopeless optimist, a person full of enthusiasm, one who jumps before I assess the size of my leap. It took many years of personal growth, however, to admit to my second affiliation—my

WITHOUT OUR DOUBTS WE WOULD FIND IT
HARD TO SHOW OUR FAITH.

likeness to Thomas. I realize that much of my reservation in acknowledging this similarity stemmed from the negative reputation that this dear man enjoys, that of expressing and showing his doubts.

It was not until I read the book *Twelve Ordinary Men*, by John MacArthur, that I began to recognize my likeness to Thomas. Instead of regarding him as doubting, I learned to see him as honest! If all of us were as forthright as he was, I believe most folk would also relate to Thomas. We can take this one step further: without our doubts we would find it hard to show our faith. For this reason, left brain thinkers who are analytical, logical critics may well have an enormous challenge when it comes to exhibiting faith. In fact most of us have been taught all our lives not to believe that which we cannot prove...QED, quod erat demonstrandum (Latin for "what has been proven"), has become a central doctrine of our education. In contrast, as the Bible tells us in Hebrews 11:1, "Faith is being sure of what we hope for and certain of what we do not see."

It has been stepping out in faith and onto God's pathway, while not seeing His reason or purpose for me to do so, that has brought me the most joy in my life. It is constantly living in a world of uncertainty, having opened up my heart and mind to God's call, that has given me the greatest peace and satisfaction. There are times when reasons or purpose are revealed; sometimes they aren't. Nevertheless, it is safe to say that every time I have stepped out in faith in response to God's call, I have been rewarded by Him in some way. Now I hunger for the intimacy that my faith walk with the Lord brings, while acknowledging the honesty of whatever human doubt that might entail. The answer to the faith/reason conundrum for me is to trust God with my doubt.

The incredible story of the wedding ring is one that, had I not been a principal participant, I would find almost impossible to believe. It was June 12, 2012, and I had just joined the other participants in the Grow Life Church Mission Team at the Orlando International Airport. We were scheduled to fly down to Miami for our connection to Tegucigalpa on our way to the City of Hope Orphanage. But as I had booked my flights at a different time than the rest of the team, my seat was located apart from them. The flight was packed, and I found myself having to sit on the floor at the gate in Miami to await boarding. I spent the time reading my book and minding my own business.

When my group was finally called, I lined up with the other folk in seats numbered 20 through 35 at the entrance to the boarding ramp. By the time I got to row 25, seats D and F were already occupied. The window seat, F, was the one I thought I had booked since I never like to sit in the middle. I was somewhat irritated to find that it was occupied. The young Hispanic woman who was sitting in it had her face firmly turned to the outside world. Seat D was taken by a good-looking young man in his mid-to-late twenties who jumped to his feet to offer to heave my carry-on luggage into the rack above. I was truly grateful to this gracious gentleman and decided that things were definitely "looking up." As I settled into the middle seat and started to sort out my reading material, I saw that I was not the only woman that my neighbor was helping. He jumped to his feet every time he noticed a single woman who needed to hoist her bag overhead, and assisted by organizing the spaces and getting the bags to fit in the over-crowded bins.

As the flight filled up and the attendants prepared us for takeoff, I detected a change in the manner of my seating companion. He fidgeted and seemed to be looking for something under his seat. His searching became frantic. "What's up?" I asked. "Anything I can do to help?"

"I've lost my wedding band," he replied, "and I have no idea when—or where it could be."

"Well, you have helped a lot of us with our bags. Perhaps it came off while you put a bag into the overhead bin." We searched around the floor but had to stop looking while the plane took off. "Try to sit down and relax for a couple minutes. What's your name?"

He looked at me, distress clear in his eyes. "Edwin," he said. "My wife is going to kill me when she finds out I've lost my ring. I knew it was a little loose and I have had a year since our wedding to get it sized properly."

"Tell me what it looks like, and we'll get the flight attendant to help out and get the other passengers to look for it as well."

When the flight attendant passed by we told her about the lost ring. She promised to make an announcement over the loud speaker once she had time later in the flight. In the meantime, Edwin couldn't relax or settle at all, and I could tell he needed help. Not having any idea about what (if any) religion or affiliation with God he might have, I leapt out in faith and suggested that we hold hands and pray. He was very receptive to the idea, so as the plane taxied the runway we communicated with God for ten to fifteen minutes. Edwin seemed more relaxed, and we were able to discuss the multiple places the ring might be. Frankly, he told me, he couldn't remember the last time he had seen or felt it. My heart sank. Now the ring could be anywhere around Miami!

The flight attendants busied themselves with getting drinks and snacks, and I began to fear that our problem had been forgotten. Edwin was obviously thinking the same thing and, when we were about an hour into the flight, he decided that he just couldn't sit still anymore. He started to search once again and I joined in.

Now our seating companion by the window was being disturbed, and she asked us what our problem was.

"Edwin's wedding ring is lost, and we are searching for it," I told her.

There was a five second pause and then a surprising response: "I think I might know where your ring is, but I'm not sure."

Neither Edwin nor I said a thing. In fact, I think my mouth had dropped open and Edwin looked frozen. Neither one of us could get a word out despite the fact that we were so desperate to ask "WHERE?" Instead we were left to her mercy to continue and, thankfully, she did.

HE RETURNED TO HIS SEAT
DISTRAUGHT AND EMPTY-HANDED,
NOT KNOWING QUITE WHAT TO DO NEXT.

"As I was waiting to board the plane at Miami, I struck up a conversation with another woman. We commented about how full the flight was going to be and how we hoped that it would be on time. We talked for at least fifteen minutes before her seat number was called to board. As she handed her boarding pass to the attendant, she noticed something on the floor and bent down to pick it up. The woman then turned and showed it to me before she headed onto the plane. I'm not sure, but I think it might have been a ring."

Edwin remained paralyzed, but I managed to catch a breath and ask the important questions.

"Did she board our plane?"

"Yes," our seating companion said.

"What does she look like?" we asked in unison.

"She is tall and slim, around 5 foot 8 inches and has short dark hair," the woman responded.

"Did you see her once you were on the plane? Do you know where she is sitting?" Edwin and I were really excited now.

"No, I haven't seen her, but I think her seat number was somewhere towards the rear of the plane. I didn't see her as I looked for my seat."

Edwin was already out of his seat, heading towards the back of the plane to find a tall, dark-haired lady. But he truly didn't have any idea what she looked like. He returned to his seat distraught and empty-handed, not knowing quite what to do next. While he was gone, I had continued my interrogation of the lady to my right, thinking how unconcerned she seemed to be. The look of frustration on Edwin's face was quite enough to give me the courage I needed.

"Please, please," I begged my neighbor, "Do you think you could walk to the back of the plane for us to see if you can spot her? This is so very important to this man."

"Yes, of course, I'll certainly try." She gathered her things and started to get up.

I leapt to my feet, allowing her a free pathway to start her search. Edwin and I stood in the aisle, not even conscious of the fact we were anxiously clasping hands and staring at her progress. She didn't hesitate; she walked straight up to a lady sitting by the window about fifteen rows back and started a conversation. There was much smiling and nodding of heads, and then our seating companion returned to us with a broad grin and a silver wedding band held high for us to see.

By the time she reached our seats, all three of us were in a flood of tears—tears of joy. It was Edwin's ring! The errant ring was once more placed safely in its rightful place on Edwin's finger and, much to amusement of the surrounding passengers, the three of us celebrated with an animated dance.

It was Edwin who asked for us to join hands to give praise and thanks to the Lord. So there we were, three total strangers brought together to play out one of God's incredible miracles, praying and giving thanks and realizing as every second passed just how many chance events had to take place for the three of us to end up sitting in one row together in order to have Edwin recover his ring.

There are some, I am sure, who will say, "What a lucky coincidence that these three total strangers ended up sitting next to each other on the plane." However, you and I know that with God there is no such thing as a coincidence; there are merely God-incidences.

When I look back on this experience, it brings me such joy and wonder, and I am filled with a deep gratitude for our awesome God. I like to feel that it was our sincere prayer of faith as the plane took off that made all the difference. Did I honestly think or know that God would help find the ring and create this incredible miracle? Quite frankly, no! Just like Thomas, I had my doubts. But I can proudly state that my faith never wavered.

"And Jesus said to him, "If you can! All things are possible for one who believes." Immediately the father of the child cried out and said, "I do believe: help me overcome my unbelief!"
Mark 9:23-24 (NIV)

CHAPTER 11: PARABLE OF THE IMPOSSIBLE TASK

"Shoot for the moon and be happy you fall amongst the stars." {Vicki Piccirilli}

THERE ARE MANY chapters in this book that illustrate trusting the outcome of a situation to the Lord, but the story where the need for faith is perhaps the most palpable is that of the dormitory construction at City of Hope.

There are many reasons for this. First, I had close to zero experience in construction, and what I did know did not apply in Honduras. Then there was the fact that construction takes money and we had none. On top of which was the added challenge of not being able to communicate in Spanish, the local language; nor did I have much knowledge of the local Honduran culture, available labor, supplies or costs. And of course we had no plan or architectural drawing. I have to admit, when first asked by Pastor Jose to help him build a new dormitory for the girls at Casa Hogar, I had little realization when saying "yes" of the challenges that were about to confront me. Obviously ignorance is bliss!

In December of 2011, I was asked by my Community Bible Study director Marilyn to speak about my missionary call to Casa Hogar, City of Hope. By that point, I had already managed to have a video presentation compiled for the new website with pictures of the children, the history, the purpose and the needs. Though the talk was to be angled more towards the teaching of the Book of Isaiah, and the fact that we need to answer God's "call" when we get it, I also recognized an opportunity to show what I was specifically being asked to do – build a dormitory. So I ended with the point that although it was seemingly an impossible task and I had absolutely no idea how to do it, the Lord had said, "Go build a dorm"!

As I left the church sanctuary after the presentation to go to my class, Dawn Lovo, the core leader of another class, came up to me. "Do you have someone to do your plans or architectural drawings? My husband and I are in the process of building our new home here in Lutz, but plans and architectural drawings is our profession. As I don't have any spare money right now, I would love to donate the drawing of the plans to you and City of Hope!"

There was already no doubt in my mind that the Lord had called me to help City of Hope, but having blatant confirmation from Him is always an awesome experience. I burst into tears of gratitude, both to God and to Dawn, and hugged this dear lady. We arranged a meeting for later in the week to discuss things together with Pastor Juan Carlos (my local link to Casa Hogar). The meeting at Café Fresco was a delight, and I think Dawn managed to gain more of a perspective on what the situation was and what the apparent needs were going to be. The first step was to contact Ali at the orphanage to see if she had any idea or plans of her own, as she was, after all, the one who would know what the greatest requirements would be. I emailed Ali in Honduras that day, and asked her to meet with Pastor Jose to discuss what they had in mind when it came to designing the new facility for the girls. I suggested making a drawing of what she envisaged, to scan and email back to us.

It only took a week for the drawing to be emailed back to us...the plan was to have a two story building with enough dormitory space on the ground floor for up to 24 children, evenly set on two different ends of the building. We needed to be able to house all the children, girls at one end and boys on the other, until the necessary repairs were completed in the building they were presently using. Ali's plan was emailed to Dawn and the architectural drawing started immediately. Dawn had actually been working on another dormitory project for a family fostering ten to twelve children, and she felt that this plan might be one Ali would be interested in as well. Both were sent to Ali when finished to give her a choice. It was Dawn's plan that Ali preferred and chose; the necessary renditions for foundation, plumbing, interior walls and beams were completed over the next few weeks and by the time I left for Honduras in March we had the complete set. What a gift from the Lord, this lovely lady Dawn Lovo was and is to us! But we weren't done with our task yet.

The mission trip to Mission Del Mar at El Porvenir in March, 2012, was a joy to every one of us who participated and there were many memorable stories; perhaps the funniest being the story of my errant tooth, which is the subject of another parable. The outcome of my "tooth" problem was that I would have to return to Mission Del Mar in April so that the dentist, Karla Planko, would be able to finish the work that was necessary to put my mouth back into order. Though it doesn't necessarily take me by surprise any more, I still am amazed at how God orchestrates events to fulfill His plans. Having to return to Mission Del Mar was one such event, as it gave me the opportunity and time needed to discuss the construction and dormitory project at City of Hope with Scott Ledford.

By the time I met them on my first short-term mission trip in July, 2011, the Ledfords had been at Mission Del Mar for six years. Six years of incredible growth and service to this poverty-stricken community of Honduras! It had become obvious that the wide variety of jobs and experience Scott had mastered earlier in his life had been for this time and purpose. They had built and enclosed extra living space at the mission itself, adding many additional beds for the ever-increasing short-term mission teams who volunteered to come and serve. Together with these teams, the couple built churches, schools, orphan-ages and homes...wherever the need was greatest. They had set up feeding stations all around the La Ceiba area. They initiated a pastoral program at the mission house to enable local men gain a theological degree and accreditation. Susan organized sewing and craft lessons to help local women start an arts and crafts program. Knowing the biggest need was to help establish income for the local folk, Scott started a boat building project to encourage fishing as a trade. He had successfully overseen local fishermen in building close to thirty of their own boats with funds of $200 per boat, donated specifically for that pur-pose.

In short, the Ledfords had become an integral part of the community and were totally immersed in its day-to-day needs, challenges, and triumphs. Scott had mastered the Spanish language and Susan had grasped enough to communicate well with her neighbors. It became quickly apparent that there was hardly anyone in the village, man, woman or child, who didn't know and love Señor Scott and Señora Susan. Their philosophy of ONE, concentrating their efforts on one need at a time and spreading the word of Christ to one person at a time, had paid bountiful dividends.

It was clear that Scott had the necessary experience and knowledge of construction that I needed to tap into in order to start the City of Hope dorm project. God had led me into Scott's life for so many reasons, but one of the most important was this initial help required to begin the task. Having discussed my challenge on my return to El Porvenir in April, the first thing that Scott did for me was to introduce me to a local young man by the name of Adonis, who had worked on many construction projects with him in the past and was someone who Scott trusted. Though I was not able to speak Spanish, the three of us managed to communicate well through Scott's translating. Dawn's drawings and plans were paramount, of course, and they gave Scott and Adonis what was necessary to give some basic direction.

Adonis agreed to return to City of Hope with me for a few days to meet Ali, to compare local costs in Tegucigalpa, and to assess the construction site first-hand. He imparted some useful advice on how to build the foundation and footer, and the dimensions that were necessary for the size and weight of the proposed building and to suit the local terrain. There were drawings of the footer, stem wall, interior walls and cement beams showing how to support the ceiling that was to be the floor to the second story. Adonis offered his services as a foreman if needed, but it was decided that a local man, Yoni, would be a much better choice as he was familiar with the local manpower and supplies that were readily available in Tegucigalpa. Yoni was also a known, loved, and trusted professional who had been used on many previous occasions by Pastor Jose and Ali at the orphanage.

It quickly became apparent that the first job needing to be done was to raise the metal gate by four feet, in order to give access to the excavator to prepare the 100' x 70' construction site. This of course also enabled the cement trucks to reach the site; and just as important, the septic tank truck that was so desperately needed to clean out the huge septic tank that hadn't been serviced in the six years Ali had been there. This important access had not been considered at the time the fencing and the gate had been built, and as the septic tank was also going to be used to service the new dormitory, access to it now became mandatory.

Adonis returned to La Ceiba after three vitally important days spent with us at City of Hope, and I will forever be grateful to both him and Scott Ledford for the invaluable help and information they so generously gave. I often wonder if the construction would ever have been started without their guidance, and I know with certainty that both these men came into our lives with God's impeccable timing.

We decided that Yoni would pick four men to work under him, and that the task of raising the gate would start immediately. The excavator would hopefully arrive mid-May to prepare the site and start on the ditches for the foundation. Now that we seemed to have a plan of action, it was left for me to wait and to pray. Psalm 127:1 was paramount in my thoughts and prayers since starting the project with Dawn back in January, and I made sure that all the plans, drawings, and in fact all the documentation involving the construction, contained the quote "Unless the Lord builds the house, those who build labor in vain," so as to remind us all who was truly in charge. Not being someone who finds it easy to be idle, I busied myself with painting Ali's bedroom and bathroom on the ground floor, and then every room of the second floor of the mission house. What fun it was to stencil scripture over each of the doorways!

It was not long before Yoni and his guys were there to start work on the gate. Yoni's son Harold spoke English, and became an invaluable help to the missionaries and myself at a later stage while we worked the construction onsite under Yoni's guidance. The gate had to be dismantled at the top, which proved a larger job than anticipated. The cross beam, built originally by Yoni as well, was re-enforced concrete, and built to last centuries! Needless to say, the children found the new activities a wonderful distraction from their normal routine, but the excitement that the arrival of cement blocks, gravel, sand, and cement prompted was truly a delight and brought joy to my soul. Our wonderful boys took it on themselves to unload and stack close to a thousand blocks ready to be used for the stem wall.

My original intention had been to stay in Honduras for a five to six month period, but I discovered that the local immigration limits visits to three months at a time. Again God's plan was a better one than mine. I returned to Tampa at the end of May, just in time for me to meet up with and help prepare a large mission team from Grow Church (my daughter Vicki's family church) for their upcoming trip to City of Hope on June 12th. I enjoyed some precious time with my family before returning to City of Hope along with this wonderful team who were to start the actual construction.

The funds collected had reached close to $30,000, a quarter of the way to our estimate and the final goal of $120,000 needed to complete the project. It was more than enough to start...so we did, knowing that the Lord would provide for each step as we got to it. When we arrived at City of Hope, we found the site prepared and ready for the footer to be poured. In fact the cement mixers were onsite and had to move out of the driveway to allow our bus with precious cargo of missionaries to unload.

The team from Grow Life was a total joy, and included both Juan and his brother Doug, who were instrumental in first introducing me to the needs at Casa Hogar. Having them with us as we started the construction project seemed like "icing on the cake"! With great enthusiasm, the team immediately set about dumping their bags and getting out on-site to start transporting the cement blocks down to the foundation area. The two general contractors on the team, Gary and Tim, checked that the footer was being done correctly and assessed the best ways in which the additional man power could be used over the following week. They had a meeting with Harold and Yoni and a plan for the week was established.

Few of us had ever worked as hard as we all did that week. We hand-carried a never ending supply of blocks one-hundred and fifty yards down to the site; sifted a continuously replenished mound of sand to "caretta" (along with the gravel) down to the mixing pad; carried 100lb bags of cement powder; hand-mixed literally tons of concrete and mortar; carried bucket upon bucket of mortar and concrete to the men working on building the stem walls, all while trying to control and empty the rain-filled trenches. By the fourth day our goal of the team completing the foundation and stem wall had been achieved and the team started to back-fill the site.

Another goal was for the team to get to know and start to relate to all the children at Casa Hogar, and this was mostly achieved by them working alongside of us on the construction site. Tim Harvey's wife, Mardee, also spent a great deal of time locked away doing projects in the sewing room for the children, and much to their delight, Krystal, Brianna and Zach would leave the construction and spend much of their time doing homework projects and games with them. None of us failed to be amazed by the strength and resilience the children demonstrated onsite, and the amount of help they gave was one of the reasons we reached our goal so quickly. I don't know how we would have coped without them, but the gift of being able to get to know and appreciate each one proved to be the greatest blessing of all. I remember recording later on the Facebook page that one of the greatest hidden benefits that the construction project has had is to teach the children how to construct a house from beginning to end!

It was not all work for the mission team, and as we were ahead of our goal on site, we decided to take Saturday (as well as Sunday) off to accompany the boys to their soccer matches. So we all piled into the orphanage van on Saturday morning to go to watch and support "our" boys. It proved to be huge fun, especially when the mission team formed a soccer team of "mature" guys and joined in the competition. The ladies abstained from playing, but the amount and vigor of our laughter created as many painful rib aches as the ones experienced by those who played soccer!

Sunday was yet another memorable day. As there were so many of us, and as we wanted to take all twenty-three children out to lunch and to Valle De Angeles after church, we had organized a large bus to do the job. The church service was wonderful with Pastor James from Grow Life giving the message, translated by Pastor Juan into Spanish for the local congregation. Giving a sermon or speech and having it translated as it is being spoken is an art form of its own. I can honestly state that I have never heard it done better than by these two wonderful men of God. There followed a mimed skit that was acted out by the entire mission team – the meaning of Jesus' love being our saving grace and all we need came through clear and strong.

Lunch in a restaurant at a local mall was enjoyed by all, but the visit to Valle De Angeles in the afternoon could not have been more wonderful. Each of the missionaries was put in charge of two of the children, and as we toured the little tourist village looking for souvenirs the bond between us all seemed to get better and better. Though they did not have much to call their own, there was not one child who asked for anything for themselves, and each had to be persuaded to receive the gift that was given with such genuine love. It was a very tired but happy bunch of folk that got back into the bus that evening to return to Casa Hogar.

Monday was the last day for the mission team, and it dawned hot and humid, having rained heavily through the night. The construction site was waterlogged, and most of our efforts were directed at trying to empty the ditches, and have the runoff avoid the little shack homes in the valley below. A complicated drainage system was devised and seemed to work well; however, the water-logged soil made the back-filling of the site exceedingly difficult and very heavy. The mission team was exhausted, which only added to the pain and stress of having to say farewell to the children that night; boys and girls who they had genuinely grown to love and appreciate had now become a part of their lives forever. Not many of the Grow Life team left without a promise to return.

As the new day dawned at 5:30 a.m. on Tuesday, I took my cup of coffee out onto the balcony that overlooked the entire property at Casa Hogar. Looking down on the construction site it suddenly struck me that we had actually started this seemingly impossible task that the Lord had given me. The foundation and stem wall were complete and the perimeter of the building was there for everyone to see. Tears of gratitude to the Lord flooded into my eyes as I began to realize the huge privilege He had bestowed on me.

I was personally very sad to see my dear friends from Grow Life leave, but they promised to take my love and the news and pictures of our progress back to my daughter and her family for

GOD IS IN THE BUSINESS OF
WORKING THROUGH HIS PEOPLE
TO ACCOMPLISH IMPOSSIBLE TASKS.

me. It was Vicki's saying, to "Shoot for the moon and be happy to fall among the stars," that had given me courage and helped me truly understand that you cannot fail if you step out in faith for the Lord, and that beyond doubt, there is nothing to fear. I had learned an important truth: God is in the business of working through His people to accomplish impossible tasks.

God helps people complete impossible tasks all throughout the Bible, but there is an obvious parallel concerning construction with the story of Nehemiah. Nehemiah was a common man in a unique position. He was a secure and successful cupbearer to the Persian king Artaxerxes. He had little power, but he had great influence because he was trusted by the king. He was also a man of God, concerned about the fate of Jerusalem.

Seventy years earlier, Zerubbabel had managed to rebuild God's temple. Thirteen years had passed since Ezra had returned to Jerusalem and helped the people with their spiritual needs. Now Nehemiah was needed. Jerusalem's wall was still in ruins, and the news broke his heart. As he talked to God, a plan began to take form in Nehemiah's mind about his own role in rebuilding the city's walls. He willingly left the security of his home and job in Persia to follow God on an "impossible" mission. And the rest is history.

From beginning to end, Nehemiah prayed for God's help. He never hesitated to ask God to remember him, closing his autobiography with these words: "Remember me with favor, O my God." Throughout the "impossible" task, Nehemiah displayed unusual leadership. The wall around Jerusalem was rebuilt in record time, using every Jewish family there and despite huge resistance. Even Israel's enemies grudgingly and fearfully admitted that God was with these builders. Not only that, but God worked through Nehemiah to bring about a spiritual awakening among the people of Judah.

God often shapes people with personality characteristics, experiences, and training that prepare them for His purpose, and usually we have no idea what God has in store for us. God prepared and positioned Nehemiah to accomplish one of the Bible's impossible tasks. Since that day on the balcony at the City of Hope, there has never been a time, while taking photos of the incredible progress on the construction site, that I don't look up to heaven to give thanks to the Lord for His ongoing faithfulness, and for giving me His impossible task.

"Unless the Lord builds the house, those who build labor in vain."
Psalms 127:1 (ESV)

Chapter 12: Parable of the Errant Tooth

"What we anticipate seldom happens;
what we least expected generally happens." {Benjamin Disraeli}

LIFE IS SIMPLE here in Honduras...or so it seems! There is much to do, but there seems no urgency in doing it. There is time to reflect, to enjoy, and to connect with God in a manner that seems somehow more difficult back home. Here He seems so close and with me at all times, showing me what it is He sees and what is important to Him. Here, I can live in a Mary world, leaving my Martha self for another day.

I remember a few years back participating in a study on "living a Mary life in a Martha world", and in all honesty I found it difficult to relate to Mary. Having been a Martha for as long as I could remember, I wanted God to show me what it would be like to be a Mary. There seemed so many valid reasons for remaining a Martha; everything in my life seemed to be urgent or important. After all, look how many people I would be letting down if I didn't get things done NOW! Then, of course, there was the achievement factor. Surely my day could not be termed successful if I didn't manage to accomplish at least half of what was on my "to do" list; a list set up the night before in priority order. Might there also have been a guilt factor? Perhaps I would get an "F" or "D" if I didn't finish my list!

I haven't lost my desire to accomplish tasks...no, it's not that. It is, perhaps, accepting that I have very little control over whether or not things get done in my timing. Here, it always seems to be in God's timing. It's not a matter of whether there is much or little to do; it's a matter of living in God's peace while we do it, and making sure we don't confuse activity with productivity.

So now we have the story of my errant tooth. To set the stage a little, I must share that I loathe going to the dentist. It is revolting to have someone else's fingers in my mouth. I detest the horrible variety of noises and the continuous fear of the shock I will suddenly feel when a nerve makes itself known. To make matters worse, the older I get, the more sensitive my teeth become. So being the coward that I am, I reason that the fewer times I visit the dentist, the better off I am.

When I joined a Thursday morning referral group from the Temple Terrace Chamber of Commerce in 2008 and found that we had a dentist member, Andi from Dr. Maya's Today's Dentistry, I knew my days of ignoring my teeth were numbered. Even so, I managed to delay the inevitable and it was February of 2011 before I actually got around to making an appointment—a full nine years since I had last allowed someone's fingers other than my own in my mouth.

I was pleasantly surprised that there was not a great deal of urgent work that needed to be done. A good and thorough cleaning, of course, was the number one priority. This was done with quick professional ease and, with a mouthful of x-rays completed, it was determined that I only had one large tooth on the bottom left that needed attending to at a later date. There was, however, an implanted tooth up top and in front that needed to be dealt with immediately. The work had originally been done in England forty-five years previously, and it had later been replaced in South Tampa on my last visit to a dentist. Since then, the tooth had been through various stages of feeling loose. The root had obviously suffered some abscess damage in the past, which created a black gum above it that I had successfully ignored. As it was unlikely that there was any bone left to make a replacement implant secure, the best treatment seemed to be a moderately simple process:

Step #1. Straighten the upper teeth that had shifted to the right in an effort to "oust" the offending tooth back to the left using braces. Dr. Leever, an orthodontist, was chosen to make the braces and two clear retainers: one to keep the teeth in place while my dentist arranged to remove the errant tooth, and a second clear retainer with a fake tooth to keep the teeth in place while allowing the gap and bone graft the necessary time to heal.

Step #2. Dr. Maya to pull the tooth and do the bone graft.

Step #3. Use the teeth on left and right to form a bridge.

The cost for Dr. Leever's orthodontic procedures was estimated at $1,500. Dr. Maya's discounted estimate for the last two steps was close to $6,700. I was not a happy camper, since

I would have to take out a loan to have this work done. *C'est la vie!* The work needed to be done, so I had best get on with it.

Everything went well until step #2, about three months into the process. It was time to have the tooth extracted. For some reason it was only now that the health history form I had completed four months previously was read. It was noticed that I had checked off von Willebrand Disease (vWD), which is a blood condition that causes problems with coagulation. This disease had never created much of a problem for me and I nearly forgot to add it to the form. In hindsight, I wish I had.

My commerce group colleague Andi discussed this "new" situation with Dr. Maya, and it was decided that discretion was the better part of valor. Before we could continue, they would need a note from my general practitioner stating that it would be fine to extract the tooth. This started months of the most irritating bureaucratic red tape imaginable. "No problem!" I'm told by Andi, "We have plenty of time to get everything done before your planned five-month mission trip to Honduras. You don't leave until March."

My primary doctor decided that he could not give the okay, and that we needed blood tests and an appointment with a hematologist to confirm that I had vWD. So I was given a referral to a Medicare-approved hematologist. No problem, we still had plenty of time (four months) to get everything done.

My visit to the hematologist revealed that blood tests ordered by primary doctor had not been adequate to give good results on von Willebrand's. Ten more blood tests were needed! A second appointment to the hematologist three weeks later revealed, of course, that *I do* have vWD, yet in a very mild form. Not mild enough to give the go-ahead on a normal dental extraction. No, the hematologist told me a night in the hospital was necessary to have a drug administered to thicken blood. This would be followed by an extraction performed by a dental surgeon because of the possible complications in stopping blood flow. The hematologist realized that we needed to speed things up; not, however, because of my impending mission trip (now two months away), but because she was going on pregnancy leave in three weeks' time.

The challenges now evolved into finding a hospital *and* a dental surgeon who were covered by Medicare, because we were talking about a medical condition, not a dental problem. On top of this, the hematologist and the general practitioner (GP) were in disagreement as to who was responsible for the negotiations with Medicare to find the professionals needed. Being more interested in soon-to-arrive babies than in my tooth, the hematologist and her staff seemed less than helpful; so Bobby, my GP's assistant, took it upon herself to do the necessary legwork. Only to find that no Medicare dental surgeons or hospitals could be found on the provider list within one hundred miles of Tampa.

As vWD is not a common disease, the folks at Medicare found it difficult to understand why I should need to be in a hospital for a simple dental extraction, which is not usually covered by Medicare. Eventually, after three weeks of discussions, Bobby managed to make them understand the situation and a dental surgeon, Doctor Levine, was chosen. An appointment was scheduled just three weeks before my scheduled departure for Honduras. Bobby started looking for an approved

GOD WAS ALWAYS IN CONTROL AND HIS PLAN WOULD BE GOOD. IT JUST NEVER OCCURRED TO ME THAT THE OUTCOME WOULD BE SO HYSTERICALLY FUNNY.

hematologist, as our original choice was happily on pregnancy leave and didn't have a hospital stand-in.

Dr. Al Hassani was chosen, and I personally paid for and satisfactorily completed both appointments with Drs. Levine and Hassani. Bobby, who now had a fond relationship with our Medicare Approval Board, continued her fight to get everyone approved. The approvals finally came in for everything, but not in time to organize the pre-op procedure and surgery by the last Wednesday (Dr. Levine's one day for in-hospital surgeries) before I left for Honduras. Now that it was clear that having the tooth extracted prior to my mission trip was not an option, I set up an appointment back at the Brace Place to have retainers made to keep me going while on my five month mission. These fabulous folk had them done and ready to pick up in one day.

As I reflect on these three months prior to leaving for Honduras, I have to admit that although my "Martha" self kept pushing to get my tooth problems resolved before leaving, I never lost hold of the understanding that no matter the outcome, God was always in control and His plan would be good. It just never occurred to me that the outcome would be so hysterically funny.

As we sat at dinner in Mission Del Mar in El Porvenir on the second day of our mission trip...the tooth fell out of my mouth! I had surreptitiously taken out the brace as we said grace, putting it in a container in my pocket, but it wasn't until I was well into the meal that I realized that the tooth was missing. It was somewhat of a relief to find that is was still safely embedded in the transparent brace, and hadn't been consumed with my food. I can genuinely say that I can't remember laughing so much or so hard. My stomach hurt, and tears rolled down my face, and it was a full minute before I could explain the reason for my hysterics to my bewildered dinner companions.

So now what?

Susan, our hostess at the mission, had recently had a great deal of dental work done by a wonderful local dentist named Karla Planko. Susan recommended I see Karla early the next day when her husband Scott could take me into town at 8 a.m., while he dropped off a construction team at their work site. This was arranged and the mission accomplished. I was back working onsite with my team by 10:30 a.m., having had blood tests done at the local hospital that revealed plenty of platelets to make a root extraction safe. A further appointment was made to have this done the following Thursday.

The root was safely and easily extracted within an hour on Thursday without even a taste of blood, and I was thrilled that Karla had filed down the errant tooth's metal screw and had stuck it back into one of my braces to wear on a daily basis for four weeks to give the wound time to heal. Arrangements were made for me to return to Mission Del Mar to have the three-tooth bridge made in the middle of April. A bus trip back to Mission Del Mar in April, two more appointments with the incredible Karla, three new teeth, and a return bus trip back to Tegucigalpa...total cost $805!

God had known all along that the best place for me to get my teeth fixed at a price that I could afford was in La Ceiba, Honduras. He had it all planned in advance, and had created the most wonderful and funny chain of events at the same time.

There are so many remarkable accounts in the Bible of God's planned timing being so apparent and critical, but my favorite one is the story of Joseph, found in Genesis chapters 37-47. Joseph was the youngest of Jacob's twelve sons, and as such seemed to be his father's preferred child. As a seventeen-year old, he had not learned the value of diplomacy and bragged to his brothers that he had a dream of them "bowing down" to him. Having had enough of his arrogance and their father's favoritism, the brothers devised a plan to be rid of the irritating Joseph. They contrived to leave him in an empty cistern to die. Before they could accomplish this dreadful purpose they met some travelling Ishmaelites passing by on their way to Egypt and sold Joseph into slavery instead. Poor Jacob was told that his favorite son had been killed, and was given Joseph's colorful but bloodied coat as proof of his son's demise.

The incredible story that Joseph goes on to live in Egypt is confirmed as truth by many sources outside the Bible. And in Genesis 45: 7-8, Joseph reveals the true reason why his brothers sent him to Egypt:

"But God sent me ahead of you to preserve for you a remnant on earth and to save your lives by a great deliverance. So then, it was not you who sent me here, but God." (NIV)

The life of Joseph reveals a series of "God-incidences" and small miracles that needed to take place in order to accomplish God's ultimate plan and protection for Israel. This story also serves to remind us that no matter what makes us question the turmoil going on in our own life, it is a thread woven in the tapestry of God's plan; and though we may have no clue as to the outcome, God's plan and purpose is always a good one.

"Delight yourself in the Lord, and He will give you the desires of your heart. Commit your way to the Lord; trust in Him, and He will act. He will bring forth your righteousness as the light, and your justice as the noonday. Be still before the Lord, and wait patiently for Him."
Psalm 37: 4-7a (ESV)

Tim Harvey

CHAPTER 13: PORTRAIT OF A BUILDER

"Just look at what God does amongst the trials."
{Ted Jeschke}

ONE OF THE benefits that I enjoy as I get older is being able to look back on my life and recognize the multitude of ways that God has micromanaged and orchestrated it. Amazingly, none of the various experiences, jobs, skills, or talents from my earlier life seem to have been wasted or left unused. A lot of these "talents" are unusual or obscure, yet they have all somehow been woven back into my life to be used again and again. Some of those incidents and events were relatively painless, some were a challenge, but they all had one thing in common – at the time, I didn't know WHY! I had no idea as to *why* I was given certain abilities and neither did I know *why* I needed to wade through so many challenges.

I have to admit that once upon a time I thought that once I became a Christian, my life might be easier. Experience as a new Christian taught me that faith in God does not guarantee safety or comfort in this world. In fact, I was soon to learn the opposite was more likely the case, as God allowed me to travel through some of the most difficult and painful periods in my life *after* I became a Christian. There is a certain comfort to be gained from understanding that God has many reasons for allowing His children to endure days of anguish and suffering, as we can sometimes be led into the false belief that we bring these onto ourselves, that we've earned them as a punishment. Sometimes this may be true, but the ultimate purpose of God's discipline is to produce His character in His children. Just like any good parent, God needs to put "fences" around His children to protect them from peril, and what might seem a hardship or difficulty, might well be God's loving hand of protection.

Another reason for God allowing suffering and difficulty into our lives is to prepare us for a better, greater service. In February of 2013, Tim Harvey shared much of his life's journey with me, including the pain and anguish that he and his family had been through not just once, but twice over recent years. As a godly and God-fearing man, it is no wonder that Tim was left to ponder...*why*.

Tim Harvey was born quarter-Cherokee in 1961, the second son to his parents living in Jacksonville, Florida. He remembers very little of his first home, as in 1963 the family moved to Tampa, and then again in 1971 to the end of a dirt road in Shady Hills, just north of the city. Here two more children, another boy and a girl, were added to the family. Tim's father was a tug boat captain and his mother a bus driver. They were hard-working folk, but neither was truly a Christian influence on him. He does remember going to church, not with his family, but with a neighbor who encouraged him to ride the church bus each Sunday to the local Baptist church. Looking back at this period of time, Tim feels that the reason he kept going was more for the tasty donuts handed out by an attractive teenage girl wearing a nice smelling perfume, than as an effort to know Christ. Nevertheless, he does remember taking John 3:16 into his heart.

Tim grew big and strong, excelling in sports throughout his school life. He was an acclaimed athlete on varsity teams for football, basketball, and baseball; he also ran track. He joined the Fellowship of Christian Athletes at school, but again, more for the social side of the club than to give praise to the Lord. High school was a happy time, made even more wonderful by the fact he met Mardee, who became his high school sweetheart and later his wife and the love of his life. Mardee graduated in 1978, and soon after Tim's graduation in 1979, the couple married. Being a great student, Mardee continued her education by studying to become a dental assistant while Tim set about making a living in order to support their new home, a rented trailer in Land O Lakes.

Some of Tim's happiest recollections are of joining his father to work on the tug boats going in and out of the Port of Tampa. He started a lawn maintenance business at the same time, and while helping a friend in construction also became proficient as a carpenter's helper.

T.J., Timothy Allen Harvey, Junior, was born on April 15th, 1981, and the young family moved from the trailer into Mardee's childhood home when her parents moved to Perry, Georgia. Samantha Kaye arrived in 1984, and the challenge of supporting his young family grew more daunting. Though neither of his parents ever had a problem with alcohol, Tim was very influenced by the heavy drinking habits of other family members, slipping comfortably into the pleasure and release from responsibility it seemed to bring. Like many struggling couples with young children, he felt greater and greater pressure, and his relationship with Mardee, who had started to attend Myrtle Lake Baptist Church, suffered to the point that Tim was fearful that his marriage might not be working.

It was at this critical time that Pastor Chuck Groover from Myrtle Lake came into his life. Chuck started to visit the bowling alley where Tim "hung out" with his cronies, and managed to become a regular face and a friend without being pushy or judgmental. Chuck would constantly invite Tim to come to his Sunday service, but like too many others, Tim's response was "your church doesn't want someone like me!" Chuck persevered, reminding Tim that Jesus' invitation was to "Come just as you are!"

Eventually Tim agreed, and it was at Myrtle Lake Baptist Church that he was baptized in 1986 and started his walk with the Lord. Christopher Norman was born the same year, and the Harvey family of five blossomed under the care of their church. Mardee and Tim eagerly threw themselves into Bible studies and life groups, gleaning as much of God's wisdom as they could. They served the church in many ways; Mardee leading in women's ministries, and for many years cooking the supper for the Wednesday night prayer meeting. Tim devoted his time to what he loved best, the youth ministry, and it was while teaching some 7th grade boys that the Lord spoke to him and told him to give up drinking. He gave up alcohol "cold turkey", and has not tasted a drop since that day. In 1987, at the age of twenty-six, Tim Harvey was made a deacon at their beloved church.

Though passionately loving Myrtle Lake Baptist, Mardee and Tim found themselves being led to plant a new church in Land O Lakes. When Pastor Bob Ownbey got sick just six months after the Lighthouse Church was formed, Tim found himself taking over the pastoral role for close to a year, giving him experience in teaching and leading in a far more challenging arena.

In the meantime, Tim's job and experience in construction was advancing and the industry was booming. By the time Hurricane Andrew hit Homestead in 1992, Tim knew he had much to offer the suffering people of South Florida. He and Mardee packed their bags and, together with their family, moved to Pembroke Pines to clean up the mess and to help put people's lives back together. While living and working in Pembroke Pines, Mardee took a class to learn massage therapy, and Tim enrolled in Northwestern Theological Seminary to further his knowledge of the Bible.

During the eighteen-month sojourn in South Florida, the family attended Pines Baptist Church which was a "missions-focused" church, and under Pastor Steve's leadership the Harveys were led onto the path of becoming missionaries. Tim and Mardee agreed to join a mission team going to Costa Rica in 1993, and though not the most experienced construction person of the sixteen folk going, Tim was asked to step up as leader. They had been told that the plan was to build pews for a church on the outskirts of Siquirres, and Tim felt moderately comfortable in leading the project. God's plan, however, was a little different. Tim and his crew found themselves onsite with merely a concrete slab, some poles, and a few trusses. Their job would mean replacing most of the rotted frame work and virtually building the church from scratch.

Making the job even more challenging was the fact that they were in the middle of the rainy season, and constant torrential rain was to be expected. Against all odds, it never rained during the daytime work hours; only at night. The local folk held a revival service every evening as it rained, Mardee learned a Spanish worship song to sing in the service, and more and more people came as the week progressed. By the end of the ten days the team managed to finish the walls and the roof that was built with a central cross throwing a constant, moving shadow into the church below.

At the beginning of 1994 the Harveys moved back to Land O Lakes, where Tim rekindled his lawn maintenance business and the family started to attend the First Baptist Church of Lutz. Shortly afterward Tim was offered a great job with the Property Appraiser's Office that would not conflict with his lawn maintenance business.

THEY WERE ONCE AGAIN BEING ASKED TO
STEP OUT OF THEIR COMFORT ZONE
AND TOTALLY RELY ON THE LORD
IN FAITH FOR HIS PROVISION.

At about the same time, Pastor Steve from Pines Baptist called to ask Tim to consider going on another construction mission trip; this time to build a church in Germany. The decision to go was not an easy one, as it had been such a short time since their trip to Costa Rica. Money was tight, and having just accepted a new job, it would mean letting his new boss know that the intention was to leave for ten days soon after starting it. After much prayer, the Lord was clear in his direction for the Harveys to make the mission trip.

They were once again being asked to step out of their comfort zone and totally rely on the Lord in faith for His provision. This time the team was to be 14-16 strong and full of competent construction specialists that included a general contractor, a master carpenter, a drywall specialist, and two electricians that Tim playfully nicknamed "Thunder and Lightning". Tim was again asked to lead the team, and it was this trip that made a pivotal difference in Tim's life. He started to realize that short-term missions were to become a constant call from the Lord and that they were to play an important part of his future life's commitment.

In the beginning of 1998, Tim and his family seemed poised for yet another big change. Samantha, their thirteen-year old daughter, started asking them to have another baby. Both Mardee and Tim were reticent to even think about such a move. They did not feel financially secure, they were trying to move into a new home, and any extra funds were going towards their current children's college funds. Samantha did not give up, however, and continued to harass her parents about adopting a baby, even to the point of giving them a contract saying that she would be responsible for her own college funds.

The promise to Samantha was that they would take the request seriously, and start praying about it. At this point the Holy Spirit started working on Mardee in regard to adoption, giving gentle nudges and signs on a constant basis. She watched a program on 60 Minutes about Russian, Romanian and Chinese orphanages, and then heard on the radio about an upcoming meeting regarding Chinese adoptions. She asked Tim to join her at this meeting, as it was being held locally.

Driving home from the meeting, Mardee asked Tim what he thought about the prospect of adopting, as she had been getting prompts from the Lord for many weeks. Tim had not even thought about it, but promised Mardee that he would pray to ask guidance. It was that night, however, that Mardee felt her Chinese baby girl was born in her heart.

Just two weeks later, while heading home and going north on Dale Mabry Highway, Tim was told by God to drive into the parking lot of his bank to see if he could refinance his home and get the necessary funds to start the adoption proceedings. He made the application then and there, leaving it to God as to whether they would get approved. There was enough equity in their home to start the procedures for the adoption, so they filled out the application and sent it off by the end of March, just two weeks after the information meeting they attended.

After mounds of paperwork, notarization, verification, and finally sending documents to China, all they could do was to wait. It was in September of 1999 that a picture of Subrina Ruby Faye was sent to them from China, a child born eighteen months previously. On November 5th they left for China to pick up their precious baby girl. Subrina, however, was not the only adopted child to come to the Harveys around this time period. Mardee had come into contact with a young lady of sixteen, Gillie Lydia, while doing community service. The girl's needs were obvious, and Mardee's heart just melted. Gillie was invited to join the Harvey family and her later adoption made her an official member and fourth child of the Harvey clan.

By 2002 the Harveys were seven strong, and Tim has to admit that it came as somewhat of a surprise that the Lord had not finished bringing children into their lives. The story of Gaige Nicolas joining the family is perhaps best told by Mardee:

> "We learned about Gaige through a young woman who had cheered with our daughter Samantha in middle and high school. Kaitlin Woijcheck, now 19, ran into us at a movie theater and asked how we were. She then asked, as if a light bulb had gone off in her head, if I thought we would ever adopt again. I said, 'Funny you should ask that question. We are in the process of completing MAPP classes (requirements for foster parenting) and are prayerfully considering adopting or foster care.' Kaitlin responded, 'Oh, Mrs. Harvey! I hope you do – because I know the perfect boy for you!'
>
> Kaitlin began to tell me about an 18-month old baby boy. Her mother, Sue, had provided respite care in the past for Gaige and his great-aunt. The aunt had just recently had to release Gaige back to the foster care system as she was a single woman with an 18-year old son and a profoundly autistic 15-year old who was becoming more aggressive towards Gaige. Gaige had some pretty serious respiratory issues, including needing breathing (nebulizer) treatments three to four times daily. After joining our family – with good, traditional eating and a healthy lifestyle – he no longer shows any signs of respiratory illness!"

At the beginning of 2003, everything seemed to be going well for the Harvey family. Tim now worked for Beaulieu of America, a large carpet manufacturing company that supplied most of the carpeting to Home Depot. Tim was in charge of the account, delivery and ordering for twenty Home Depots in the Tampa region, as well as running a business for doing the installations. He was well-paid and his family was reaping the benefits.

One fateful day late in 2003, Tim fell across a metal beam in a Home Depot Store, badly injuring three vertebrae in his back and messing up his knee. There followed three years of agony, immobility, and total inability to work, without even the capability of walking. From two highly ruminative jobs, Tim and his family now had to exist on worker's comp. Three years is a long, long time! Needless to say, all their savings, boat, holiday funds, and assets disappeared, and it was touch-and-go whether they would retain their home. The love and support that was poured on them by their church kept them going, and Tim's men's group at Grace Family repaired their old truck that they so desperately needed.

After years of trying all the alternatives, Tim's doctors decided that an operation was going to be needed, and they suspected that a vertebrae fusion was the answer. Tim was at the point that he didn't care, as long as they did something to help with the excruciating pain. The operation turned out to be a huge success; the vertebrae did not need fusing, the nerves and spinal cord were cleaned, and the discs trimmed. Rehab seemed moderately quick as Tim enjoyed the ease that the relief from three years of pain gave him. On his feet and finally able to get back to work, Tim was given a great position as Vice President of Sales and Marketing for a large construction company in the Tampa area. With diligence and perseverance and continuous hard work, Tim was able to build up his family resources once again, regaining much of what was lost.

Two years later Tim took the huge step of getting his own general contractor's license, something he wished he had done many, many years before. Once successfully through the exam, he opened up his own construction company, Legacy Building and Contracting, all while continuing to work in his sales and marketing position.

THERE ARE TIMES WHEN TRIALS SEEM TO BE
WITHOUT MEANING AND WITHOUT END.
IT IS AT THIS POINT THAT OUR FAITH IS
MOST SEVERELY THREATENED.

The church they were currently attending "birthed" a new church in 2009 in the Wesley Chapel area, very near to where the family lived. Once more the Harveys made the difficult decision of following the Lord's call to move their church home, becoming charter members and helping Pastor James and Grow Life Church get established.

Things seemed to be looking up again...that is until 2009. One day in April he came into his office and tripped over a paper shredding machine, crashing across a desk and hitting the floor. In the process, he badly injured his shoulder, resulting in many more months of horrible pain and being unable to work. This time the ramifications seemed even worse, with the family once again losing everything and coming within a hairs-breadth of losing their home. The construction industry was suffering the worst economic challenge in memory, and it came as little surprise that Tim was "let go" from his job. The family struggled on from day to day, wondering how they would pay the next bill, or where the money would come from in order to buy the food they needed.

Though never criticized or questioned by his family, Tim began to feel like a failure. With his injured shoulder and lack of job opportunities, he started to truly wonder what it was that the Lord was trying to teach him, and he reached the point where he found himself beyond prayer and driving around in his truck, crying like a lost two-year old. There are times when trials seem to be without meaning and without end. It is at this point that our faith is most severely threatened.

Tim contacted their mortgage company in an effort to come to an arrangement or to see if they qualified for a loan modification, but he hit a brick wall and could not reach anyone of influence. Things looked hopeless as their mortgage payments fell further and further behind.

Once more Tim managed to drag himself up from the depth of despair. Working his way through pain and disappointment, slowly his Legacy Construction business started to take flight. Tim found that even through the disastrous economic months that were choking the industry as a whole, he managed to secure some great projects that enabled him to employ others and to start getting himself back on his feet.

In July 2011, Tim was once more called to go on a mission trip, this time with the Grow Life team to construct a wall around The Life Village in Uganda. Mardee stayed at home, but friends and family raised the money to send Tim, knowing how much he was going to be needed. The trip was a success and once more Tim was assured by God that he was where he needed to be.

On his return, Tim's business continued to improve, but not to the point of his being able to catch up on his delinquent mortgage and he didn't feel he would be able to save his home. The Harveys and all their friends and family knew they could do nothing but pray. The Lord intervened. Ted Jeschke, a friend of Tim's, was at a mortgage convention and managed to speak to the Freddie Mac Rep, Bruce Clark. After hearing the Harveys' story, Bruce gave his telephone number to Ted and told him to have Tim call him. They filled out reams of paperwork and said another prayer. Then, interspersed with constant calls to the understanding and supportive Bruce, weeks and weeks of waiting began.

When the call went out for construction volunteers to go on a mission trip to City of Hope Orphanage in Honduras in June 2012, both Mardee and Tim were ready and willing, though they had not yet heard if they could keep their own home in Wesley Chapel. Once more they put the need of others in front of their own, and once more their friends and family made their mission trip possible. I met the Grow Life Mission team as they prepared for their trip a week before departure. When flying over to Honduras with the team I knew very little about this brave and faith-filled couple, but somehow I knew that they were very special, and would become a more involved and more important part of my life.

Just after returning from this mission trip to Honduras, Tim and Mardee finally heard from their bank...they had been approved. The unpaid back payments were added to the loan principle, and the new payments were reduced to something in line with what the struggling family could afford. The agreement was even better than they had dreamed possible. Tim called his great friend Ted to tell him the good news, and will always remember his words: "Just look at what God does amongst the trials!"

As with many of God's children who have come through days and years of trials and anguish, the Harvey clan is grateful for the lessons learned. They have no doubt that God uses hardship in order to prepare us for the future He has planned for us. It just now remains to be seen what that might look like for Tim and his wonderful family. One lesson learned is that God might not prevent more trials and challenges from coming into their lives, but they can all rest on the assurance that God, just as He did with the Israelites wandering in the desert, will provide for their needs.

In the meantime Tim and Mardee remain committed to their missionary work. They have already made two more trips to Honduras since their initial one in 2012, and Tim continues to give invaluable assistance to the construction of the new dorm at City of Hope. He and Mardee hope to take Subrina with them on the next mission trip, planned for June of 2013.

I am also delighted to report that on May 28, 2013, Tim will become the first ever inductee into the Land O Lakes High School athletic Hall of Fame.

"We know that for those who love God all things work together for good, for those who are called according to His purpose."
Romans 8:28 (ESV)

"He has said, 'I will never leave you nor forsake you.' So we can confidently say, 'The Lord is my helper; I will not fear; what can man do to me?'"
Hebrew 13:5b-6 (ESV)

CHAPTER 14: PARABLE OF FORGOTTEN SKILLS

"Your talent is God's gift to you. What you do with it is your gift back to God." {Leo Bascaglia}

AFTER THE Grow Life Mission Team left Casa Hogar to go back to Tampa, life normalized and was considerably less busy at the orphanage. Though I helped out on the construction site every day by sifting the sand for the mortar, my focus turned more to helping with the children as much as I could, as Ali was so very busy. My help was very limited because I still couldn't speak Spanish fluently. I had started to understand a little more of what was being said, but by the time I had figured it out, and what a suitable reply might be...the conversation had moved on!

One of the little boys had managed to get himself banned from the local school, and it was necessary to make sure that he was kept from spending his life out on the construction site (which is where he wanted to be of course), and confined to the dining room area to do his school work there by himself. My efforts in trying to teach him had the added benefit of making me more familiar with some useful Spanish vocabulary. So did my next task.

As a former dancer and choreographer, the compilation of dances Pastor Jose asked me create was not too much of a challenge. However, trying to teach the two dances I had choreographed, with my limited Spanish, to the six girls who were to perform at a celebration for their church in September was difficult. There was only one evening a week that didn't conflict with other activities, and as my Spanish directions were pretty pathetic, getting the girls to learn the steps and formation was not an easy task and took far longer than I expected. It seemed like we had a lot of time to begin with, but I was due to leave Casa Hogar and travel up to La Ceiba at the end of July. The Ledfords were going on a much-needed three week vacation to Paris and I had promised to help out at Mission Del Mar in their absence.

By the time I left for La Ceiba, the construction at Casa Hogar had reached the point where all the exterior walls were complete and the crew had started on the footings for the interior walls. A team from Rockledge Presbyterian Church was due to fly in at the end of August and included a missionary experienced with laying underground plumbing pipes, which was the next step in our construction process. Alicia was flying home to California in the middle of August for a three week vacation herself, so I promised to extend my own stay in Honduras another week in order to be there for them and do the necessary driving to the ferrateria (hardware store). Luckily, while growing up in the UK I had learned to drive stick shift, and continued to do so for thirty years before moving to the States; so driving the old red Tacoma truck at the orphanage was not a problem. In fact, I loved it! Negotiating the horrendous roads and traffic in Tegucigalpa was a different matter, requiring much courage and assertiveness.

While in La Ceiba, I was befriended by Ceasa, a wonderful taxi driver who couldn't speak English, but seemed to be able to understand my dreadful attempts at Spanish quite well. He was thrilled to take me on tours of the area, and even drove me to the local jail in order to purchase a hammock. This was quite an experience, as we had to drive through a pineapple plantation and up to the base of the mountains in order to get there. There was no road, just a track, and I have to admit to feeling a little scared – especially when my guide pointed out the guard posts up in the trees above the compound, manned by aggressive-looking military anxious to show off their firing ability on any errant behavior below.

As we headed towards the jail compound, we drove by many women carrying and walking with children. I was told by my guide that these were the wives and families of the inmates bringing much-needed provisions for their spouses who would otherwise have to survive, as the less fortunate inmates, on two small bowls of beans and rice per day.

The shabby conditions of the facility were painfully noticeable, and the fenced compound was teaming with live bodies, all clamoring to get near to the fence to sell their goods, see their families, or just "goggle" at the visitors. I seemed to draw quite a lot of attention, primarily because I wasn't Honduran, and also because I had money to spend! Seeing how well the hammocks had been made, and knowing just how much the inmates needed the money, I felt guilty for not being able to buy more than one; but I needed to save some money to buy fabric for my dancers at Casa Hogar.

Later in the week Ceasa drove me into town to a wonderful fabric store. There was a great choice of materials, but I had to stick to my budget. I decided on some lovely white seersucker fabric that was on sale and some satin in green, orange, blue, and red for the sashes. I had taken four years of dressmaking in high school, and having been quite a seamstress in the past I was able to make up my own pattern and accurately assess the amount of fabric we'd need. Susan Ledford had given me permission to use the sewing machine at Mission Del Mar and once back at the mission I was able to start on the first prototypes, making two or three patterns in an effort to give Ali and the girls at least a limited choice. I was pleased with the results and emailed photos to Ali down in Tegucigalpa for them to make a decision, since she was not going to be around when I got back and I would only have a couple of weeks to finish them before leaving myself.

Upon my return to Casa Hogar, I was delighted to find that the Rockledge team were wonderful, hardworking, and God-fearing folk. I was so thrilled to meet Jennifer Forrester, who had been visiting the orphanage for six years, and she was able to give me a lot of insight as to what the children and the facility were like originally (even before Ali's arrival). I also got to know Harry Prosser, who owned a plumbing and irrigation company in the Melbourne area of Florida. He had managed to email a list of some of the items that he was going to need for the plumbing so I could purchase them ahead of time and avoid wasting any precious work time onsite. Marv Stone had flown down from North Carolina to be with the team; he was another missionary who had been faithfully visiting the orphanage for many, many years. His love for each child was evident and inspiring and it was a privilege to be introduced to him.

The underground plumbing went well, but it was a lot of work and too much to complete in the five days the team had allowed themselves; so when I flew back to Tampa with most of the Rockledge team, we left Harry, who had extended his stay, to complete the work with Marv. I had managed to rehearse the dance with the girls to the point where I knew they could manage with practicing on their own. All the dresses had been measured, cut, and sewn together – then fitted to each child's needs.

Saying goodbye to the children was harder than I anticipated, but I promised to return in November with the Cypress Point Team, leaving envelopes with money for the upcoming birthdays – a tradition I had started that first September visit, a visit that seemed so long ago, but was truly not even a year.

As the plane took off to fly over the mountains, I was able to reflect on the last year of my life as a missionary to Honduras. I had learned so many new lessons, had been given so many new abilities, met so many new friends, and had met so many new challenges. However, the most amazing point was that the Lord had used and resurrected so many old skills that I had forgotten or assumed gone from my life.

The experience reminded me of the life of Moses, who could have been considered middle-aged by the time the Lord reused his skills, for a better purpose. He had spent his childhood and youth as a privileged member of Pharaoh's household, in fact treated as a son, being well-educated and learning leadership

THERE HAS AT ALL TIMES BEEN A REASON
FOR HIM TO HAVE GIVEN US OUR SKILLS,
TALENTS, CHALLENGES, AND EXPERIENCES –
WE JUST NEED TO BE WILLING
FOR HIM TO USE THEM.

skills in order to help lead the Egyptian Empire. He ended up killing an Egyptian who was mercilessly beating a Jew, one of his own people, and had to flee from Egypt across the desert to Midian in order to escape Pharaoh's wrath and certain death. He married the daughter of a priest in Midian and had a family by the time God revealed himself in a burning bush to give instructions for Moses to go back to Egypt to free the Israelites from bondage and lead them to the Promised Land. Luckily the original Pharaoh had died, but Moses still needed a great deal of courage in order to return to Egypt.

The ten plagues were a tool that God used in order to get Pharaoh to release the Israelites, but then it was Moses' education, leadership skills, and survival experience that the Lord used to guide His Chosen People as they traveled through the desert for forty years.

In truth, the Lord uses anyone, any circumstance or experience, to suit his Plan and purpose; but it never fails to amaze me how His plan has always been there, from before creation and through eternity. It is wise to recognize that there has at all times been a reason for Him to have given us our skills, talents, challenges, and experiences – we just need to be willing for Him to use them. There is nothing like the feeling of joy when forgotten abilities and talents get resurrected to make you eternally grateful to the Lord for the details of your life. The understanding that so much of my former life, passions, and skills were given to me for this very time and place both humbled me and brought me overwhelming joy.

"The Lord of hosts has sworn: As I have planned, so it shall be, and as I have purposed, so shall it stand."
Isaiah 14:24 (ESV)

Mimi

CHAPTER 15: PORTRAIT OF A BROKEN HEART

"For the sorrowing Christian, the scriptures and the Lord's work serve to comfort the grieving person's spirit, body and soul. If loss has visited you, take the weapons God provides grieving hearts; His Word and work." {Jewel Johnson}

DICTIONARIES DEFINE GRIEF as deep and intense sorrow or distress; acute mental anguish. One takes for granted that grief is brought on by the death of a loved one, but actually grief is triggered by the loss of anything held precious. It doesn't necessarily have to be a death; it can be a divorce, a child leaving home, the household pet that is lost or has run away, the loss of a favorite toy, the end of a dream. In other words, simply a broken heart. In Mimi's case, it was the loss of her innocence and femininity, snatched from her while still a small child.

Mimi was born in Miami in 1966. Her mother came from Honduras and her father was Cuban. Unfortunately, though her parents professed to be Catholics, Mimi had an abusive family life that included lack of love, yelling, and discipline that

IT DID NOTHING BUT PROVE TO HER THAT
HER SIN AND TERRIBLE TRANSGRESSION
WOULD FOREVER BLOCK HER FROM HAVING
A RELATIONSHIP WITH A STRICT AND
UNFORGIVING GOD.

involved many beatings and being thrown into a closet for long periods of time. On top of this, and from a very early age, she was constantly sexually abused by a business associate of her mother's. Mimi was terrified to say anything because of the threats he made.

Continuous ill treatment through childhood and being raped through her middle school and high school years had the inevitable outcome of giving Mimi desperately low self-esteem. This brought on the need to cut herself. Cutting herself was something that seemed to give her relief from the pain of her life. Her high school years continued to be a nightmare, and she tried to improve them by turning to drugs.

Life didn't improve, and eventually Mimi's parents divorced; she and her brother were pushed back and forth between two homes. Her sister remained with her dad. Her mother soon remarried and her stepfather would ask the children to leave each weekend. Sometimes they found themselves with nowhere to go.

At the age of sixteen Mimi visited her mother's family in Tegucigalpa, Honduras, during the Pope's visit to the Catholic Cathedral. She vividly recalls witnessing thousands of pilgrims making their way up the steep hillside to the beautiful buildings on bleeding knees, or beating their bodies and inflicting nasty wounds on themselves in an effort to have their sins and digressions forgiven and in order to be purged and given access to God.

It did nothing but prove to her that she was incapable of earning forgiveness for herself; that her sin and terrible transgression would forever block her from having a relationship with a strict and unforgiving God. She decided to turn her back on what she perceived as religion and continued her life dulling the inner pain in the only way she knew how: cutting and drugs.

Mimi left high school without graduating and struggled on alone for seven years, until she managed to get a job working at a rental complex. The mother of one of her student tenants reached out to the troubled Mimi. This precious lady invited Mimi into her home and into her heart, teaching her what the true love of Christ looked like. It was this Christian lady that showed Mimi that there was a lot more to the world than the continuous abuse and suffering that she had tolerated for as long as she could remember; that there was a wonderful book of truth that spoke of a loving and forgiving God who wanted to have a friendship and loving relationship with her, and that it was His Son Jesus who came to the earth to teach us how we should really live our lives and enable us to be at one with God.

This adoptive family fixed Mimi's ailing vehicle, and she was encouraged to study the Bible and work hard and with integrity. She began to grow to love and respect herself while slowly getting her life back into order. After a while, she was able to move into her own apartment and start on an independent track. Mimi found that property management was indeed her forte, and it was something she truly enjoyed. She managed to overcome some of her hard-earned distrust and came to enjoy the interaction with people that her job permitted and encouraged. Now away from her Christian family, however, Mimi started to fall back into her former bad habits. She started again as a "social" drug user.

In 2002 the Lord once more intervened in Mimi's life in a major way. She was at work in her office and heard a heated discussion arise in the neighboring room. She went in to see what was going on. Her co-worker pointed at the husband of one of the employees and said, "His shirt says 'Ask me about the gospel' and I am asking him but he can't answer me."

All of a sudden, and out of nowhere, Mimi started sharing the gospel. Words flowed freely and forcefully, words long forgotten from a distant past, relating the lessons she had learned so many years before while living with the Christian family and attending church. But she soon realized that she was speaking with far greater authority and with way more knowledge and insight than she truly possessed. The Holy Spirit had come into her and had given her awareness, and an understanding and strength of conviction that she'd never experienced before. Her audience sat silent, spellbound by her words and her command of the scriptures. Several minutes passed before she realized what had happened, and she went back to her office to sit down, dumbfounded.

Shaken by the experience, she decided to pack up and head for home as it was already way past closing time. Her co-worker was also her roommate so they left together. Once in the car she said to Mimi, "I've known you for a long time and I have never heard you mention G-d. Where in the world did this come from?" Mimi's memories had already started to flood back into her mind. She was replaying her life in her mind in reverse. All of a sudden she just looked at her friend and said, "I used to be a Christian." Her friend put her hand up and said, "Oh no! Do NOT talk to me about the J-word!"

Mimi just ignored her; all she could think of was that there had to be a Bible in the house. After a brief search inside the house, she headed out to hunt in a shed in the backyard. There is was, battered and discolored, but still readable. Mimi started to read as someone with a voracious appetite that must be appeased. Close to two weeks later she recommitted her life to the Lord.

Mimi sank further and further into God's word, finding peace and joy like never before. The change in her did not go unnoticed by her roommate, who grew more irritated and uncomfortable with each day and started to attack the Bible, the gospel and its authenticity. Mimi was wise enough to realize that it would not be her own ability that would change her friend's heart, so she set a challenge to read God's word first, before making sweeping statements of distrust. Her friend took the challenge and in the process, much to Mimi's great joy, eventually saw the truth in the words she was reading and converted to Christianity as a Messianic Jew. They were now able to share their faith and enjoy life as fellow Christians and did so until Mimi's roommate, a friend for eternity, moved out to get married in 2004.

Mimi dedicated her life to serving Christ, throwing herself into church life in every way possible. It all helped her rapid growth in the Word and obtaining the productive and blessed life Christ wanted for her. Mimi's life is a reflection of that wonderful scripture found in Philippians:

"And I am sure of this, that he who began a good work in you will bring it to completion at the day of Christ Jesus." Philippians 1:6 (ESV)

Mimi loved it all, but the most fulfilling and meaningful ministry for her personally was missions. Her love and affinity for those who are weak, oppressed, and unable to fend for themselves still leads her around the world, in the hope that her efforts might just make the difference needed in their lives and in obedience to the instructions given by her beloved Christ.

By the time that I met Mimi, her broken heart had healed and she was enjoying her vigorous life to the fullest, devoting every second of her free time to church and missions. She was already a veteran missionary, having served in Haiti, Peru, and Israel, as well as Honduras. She visited and took City of Hope orphanage under her wings; much of her efforts now include raising funds and finding sponsors who will purchase gifts each Christmas for the children that the world seems to have forgotten.

It is her generosity and love for the children at City of Hope that brought Mimi into my life. Getting to know her has been both a privilege and an honor. My life has become so much richer now she has become a part of it, and I look forward to the continued joy our friendship brings, and to perhaps writing her next parable...the Parable of a Mended Heart.

"I can do all things through Christ who strengthens me"
Philippians 4:13 (ESV)

Chapter 16: Parable of Purpose

"Life has no meaning. Each of us has meaning and we bring it to life. It is a waste to be asking the question if you are the answer." {Joseph Campbell}

IT NEVER FAILS to surprise me how many people live their lives without thought for the purpose of their existence. Surely understanding the meaning of life is necessary to living a fulfilling one; finding significance and purpose not only helps us navigate the challenges that arise, but encourages us to reach the goals and aspirations that make life meaningful. Conversely, many people search a lifetime for their purpose, spending their existence traveling to seek other's wisdom, delving into scholarly philosophy and attending erudite seminars; yet never find the answer they look for.

For me, it was comforting to know that I fell in the latter category – at least I was searching! It wasn't until I read Rick Warren's book *The Purpose Driven Life*, however, that I started to understand the answer. It is such a hard pill to swallow, but it isn't until you fully come to realize that "It's not about me!" that you start seeing your life in the right perspective. For many days after my first mission trip, I couldn't figure out why I felt so happy and so content. I had served others in and around my church and home many times, and I was pleased and delighted

PEACE DID NOT MEAN SLEEPY INACTIVITY!
IT MEANT THE COMFORT OF KNOWING
THAT I WAS DOING EXACTLY WHAT GOD
MEANT ME TO BE DOING.

to do so – but this was different. It was more like fitting into a really comfortable pair of shoes; shoes that made me feel like I was light and worry free, focused to do the tasks in front of me without the stress of getting it done; in other words, I felt *peace*.

Peace did not mean sleepy inactivity! It meant the comfort of knowing that I was doing exactly what God meant me to be doing; living my life to the fullest *today*, and using today to make a difference. In Ecclesiastes 3:1-8, one of my favorite passages, the Bible tells us there is a season for everything under the sun. It had been my season to take to the skies, go to Honduras, and do what I could, no matter how small, to help God's people. Digging "poop-pits" (Honduran septic systems), mixing concrete and mortar by hand with a shovel, and carrying heavy cement blocks was incredibly hard work...and something I would never have dreamed of doing back in the States. However, here in Honduras where there was little other option at an accessible price (free), it made sense and it made a difference. Each day I was exhausted yet at total peace. Each day gave me the opportunity to share the love of Christ with other locals who were working along with me, and the families we were trying to help.

I slipped back into my former life and world in Tampa at the beginning of September, thrilled to look after my grandsons while my daughter and her husband Pickles went to Monaco on an all-expenses-paid vacation that Mary Kay had awarded Vicki for her previous year's accomplishments. Being thrown back into the hustle and bustle of life in the U.S. was a jolt to my system, but the fact that I had hot water showers made up for it. It's strange that, apart from family, small basics are what you miss most while on missions. As I busied myself with the task of gaining financing for my next trip in November, and raising funds for the construction costs at City of Hope, I began sensing the Lord was pushing me in a different direction. Ali was to have her daughter and son-in-law join her soon after our mission trip in November, so the need for physical help at Casa Hogar was not so pressing; the greatest need and focus for my mission seemed to be getting money to finish the new dorm.

My mission for this new season seemed to have shifted from Honduras to touring the States in an effort to fund the construction. It was evident that my ability to travel to churches around the country to speak on behalf of our need was more useful than my hands on the ground. With dormitory construction in process and only partially funded, finishing this book as a tool to be able to use at these functions was becoming more critical. I set about contacting my editor, Julie Gabell, who had worked on my first book with me. I started to send some of the finished stories to her, with a promise to visit in the near future.

Only a couple of weeks passed before I was able to get over to see Julie where she lives in Bayonet Point. We spent a wonderful couple of hours catching up with our lives and going over what we needed to accomplish with the book. Julie is now in her seventies, and she has lived one of the most interesting lives, part of it as a nun. As I left her I was confident that the book would get well underway soon, and our goal to get the book finished and ready for publishing by the July/August 2013 time frame seemed attainable.

October came and passed rapidly, and I found myself with just a few days to prepare for my next mission trip. Both Renea Harris and I had been busy with various fundraising events; Renea had made some truly lovely paper jewelry and was busy selling it at our church and at other events, I rallied my wonderful "tea room ladies" to help with a pancake breakfast, and then Renea and I ran a holiday silent raffle at the church. What a great way to raise funds...so much fun! By the time we left for Honduras we had managed to raise $5,000 to take with us towards the construction costs for the new dormitory. Our wonderful Cypress Point Community Church team was eight members strong and included Pastor Dean, our head pastor from CPCC. Our goal was to finish off the concrete slab of the ground floor that had been started by Tim Harvey's Grow Life team just preceding us, and for Joyce Owens and her daughter Rhonda to paint a mural on the wall in the mission house.

Our mission trip was a great success. Those working on the construction site were totally exhausted each evening, as we mixed the concrete by hand and carried it in buckets into the structure to be poured – bucket by bucket – onto the floor of each room. We reached our goal of finishing the slab, and then started to help the local workers finish off the inside pillars and prepare for the next phase: building the reinforced concrete beams that would go along the whole perimeter of the 80' x 40' building, across the tops of all the walls, and across the main living room ceiling.

Excitement was bubbling at City of Hope as they prepared for the arrival of Adriana and Rick, due to start their lives with the children after Thanksgiving. Two more mission teams were also scheduled to arrive – one to celebrate Christmas with them and one to follow closely at the beginning of February. Mimi, of the Parable of the Broken Heart, was also expected during the first part of December in order to bring money from her "Christmas Drive" for the children to be able to shop for themselves and for the others at the orphanage. I was pleased to learn that the website I had developed was proving invaluable as a tool for her folk to easily make donations.

Sadly, I was leaving before Rick and Adriana's arrival, but promised the children I would try to return with Tim Harvey, our general contractor from Grow Life Church, in February.

Once again, I could leave feeling peace in the knowledge that God was in charge and would take care of the details.

Jesus gives us the secret to this inner peace after the Sermon on the Mount, found in Matthew 6:52-34, when he tells us not to worry. In the busy, complicated lives that we live nowadays this truly is easier said than done. But the key is found in verses 33 and 34: we are to "Seek first the kingdom of God and His righteousness, and all these things [talking of the former list of things that cause anxiety] will be provided for you. Therefore do not worry about tomorrow, because tomorrow will worry about itself. Each day has enough trouble of its own." Jesus is teaching us to go to God with our problems—that we should focus on what is happening in the present moment. Tomorrow not only has its own challenges, but anticipating them just makes today's fears far worse!

I have observed that my worrying yesterday about the issue that is happening today has never, ever, helped it. That is not to say that Jesus doesn't want us to be pro-active, to plan ahead; he certainly encourages us to be diligent, work hard, have goals, and make provision for tomorrow. There is a subtle difference between having concern for and being prepared for challenges, compared to worrying about a disaster to come. No, he is talking about those basic problems that are beyond our control, like future illness in the family, accidents that may happen, whether we will be struck by an earthquake or other natural disaster, our plane crashing, a relative or friend dying, or the power going out during the Super Bowl; there are a million things that play on our mind but that we have no power over.

Our specific purposes in life are many and varied, but if we hold fast to some great biblical principles we are assured of being who it is that God would want us to be. I have also been encouraged by these quotations to focus on what is important:

"We should try to leave the world a better place than when we entered it. As individuals we can make a difference, whether it is to probe the secrets of nature, to clean up the environment, to work for peace and social justice, or to nurture the inquisitive, vibrant spirit of the young by being a mentor and a guide." Michiu Kaku, theoretical physicist.

Along the same lines are the instructions given to Edward Bok, founder of Bok Tower and Sanctuary, by his grandmother as he left his home country in the Netherlands: *"Make you the world a bit better or more beautiful because you have lived in it."*

"Be very careful, then, how you live – not as unwise but as wise, making most of every opportunity, because the days are evil. Therefore do not be foolish, but understand what the Lord's will is." Ephesians 5:15-17 (NIV)

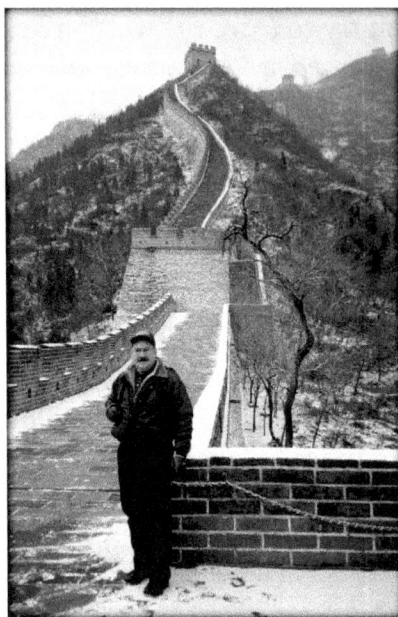

CHAPTER 17: REFLECTIONS FROM A TRAVELER

BY OMAR C. GARCIA | MISSIONS PASTOR
KINGSLAND BAPTIST CHURCH | KATY, TEXAS

"The truth is that every advance that we make for God and His cause must be made at our inconvenience." {A.W. Tozer}

MY HEROES HAVE always been travelers. Simply defined, a traveler is someone who goes beyond. I come from a family of travelers — from the 16th century, when my ancestors traveled from Spain to the New World, to the present generation. Travel is in my DNA.

As a result, I am consumed by wanderlust: that strong urge to wander and to explore and to connect with those who live beyond my familiar borders. I have never been completely satisfied staying still or staying close. My heart is tuned in to the frequency of exploring and experiencing other places.

As a kid, I loved the nights when my dad would set up his projector to show us his black and white slides of places he had visited and the people he had met on his journeys. I loved listening to his stories of traveling light and of visiting places I would later read about in school books. But, best of all, I loved his stories about making connections with people. The people in his photos gave context and meaning to the places he had visited and were always more interesting to me than buildings and landscapes.

I also enjoyed receiving packages sent from overseas by traveling family members. It was like Christmas all over again whenever a package arrived. I had to examine every detail...the stamps, the handwriting, the weight. And then, with measured restraint, I would open the package. The gifts I received gave me the edge at show-and-tell in elementary school: a leather wallet from Egypt, a small lapis-lazuli stone from Asia, a Chinese box, and even a vial of water from Antarctica.

My imagination was also stirred by the stories I heard around the dinner table and at family gatherings. My grand-parents' large home was the repository for treasures collected from years of travel. I've often told friends that I was raised in a museum. And, I was. Every room in their home was spiced with the flavor of travel in its decor. More importantly, I knew the story behind each item on the walls and on the shelves.

I also learned about the nations by perusing the photos my family kept in albums and old shoeboxes, the kind of photos with serrated edges and later those first Kodak color photos that had the date stamped along the border. I was fascinated. The best part was looking at the people who lived beyond my small South Texas town. These photos helped me to begin to understand the bigness, beauty, and diversity of our world.

Today, I am grateful to be the beneficiary of my family's legacy of travel. However, as a follower of Jesus Christ I am especially fortunate to travel with a purpose. My passion for going beyond is fueled by the last command of Christ. I love

IF WE ARE TO GROW, WE MUST GO BEYOND.
WE MUST STEP BOLDLY ACROSS THE LINE IN
ORDER TO ADVANCE THE INTERESTS OF
GOD'S KINGDOM IN OUR WORLD.

making connections with the people who live at the other end of the Great Commandment and the Great Commission.

I have discovered that the greatest adventures await those who go beyond, those who go to the farthest edge of everything they know and then take an additional step. The rewards of new friendships and exciting discoveries are found on the other side of risk and await those who are willing to lose sight of the shore. Losing sight of the shore is essential to our own growth and also to the growth and advancement of God's kingdom.

As a missions pastor, I adopted the words "Go Beyond" as the brand for the missions ministry I lead. I chose those words because I believe that in each of our lives there is a line that marks the farthest we've ever been or the most we've ever done for God and His purposes. On one side of that line is the familiar, convenient, manageable, comfortable, and predictable. No big surprises, no daunting challenges, no uncharted territory. Crossing that line, however, requires a commitment to venture to places we've never been and the willingness to engage people we've never met.

Going beyond is not always easy and often involves risk. Only those with the courage to overcome their fears and who have the determination to persevere will dare to cross that line. All others will keep a safe distance away from it. If we are to grow, however, we must go beyond. We must step boldly across the line in order to advance the interests of God's kingdom in our world.

Over the years, I have heard people remark about how they long to be a part of something exciting and miraculous for the kingdom of God, only to watch them aggressively avoid the context in which these things happen. We must be willing to place ourselves in a setting where we will see God work in and through us in new and exciting ways, in ways we never imagined. We must be willing to spend ourselves for God and His purposes and to work toward the day when the earth will be filled with the knowledge of God as the waters cover the sea. Only then will we experience the exciting and miraculous things that happen on the other side of the line.

Going beyond requires that we travel — whether that journey is across the room, across the street, or across the world. Travel has undoubtedly enriched my life. But meeting people and making friends around the world have made the greatest difference in becoming who I am. Mark Twain said, "Travel is fatal to prejudice, bigotry, and narrow-mindedness — all foes to real understanding. Likewise, tolerance, or broad, wholesome charitable views of men and things cannot be acquired by vegetating in our little corner of the earth all one's lifetime." I could not agree more!

Jesus calls us to be travelers. So, become a traveler. Be willing to forsake convenience and comfort in order to engage in kingdom initiatives. Take those first steps that will move you across the room or across the globe in order to make meaningful connections with others for the sake of God's kingdom. Go beyond!

"Jesus said to them again, 'Peace be with you. As the Father has sent me, even so I am sending you.'"
John 20:21 (ESV)

CHAPTER 18: PARABLE OF THE TEDDY BEAR

"Miracles can only happen when you get rid of the concept of 'impossible' and allow yourself to experience the magic of knowing." {Wayne Dyer}

LOOKING BACK OVER my life from that wonderful day when God seemed to first walk into my life, I can see just how much a part of my journey He has been over the past twenty years. Recently however, as I walk the path of a missionary, I see that the Lord has *always* been a part of my life. I just hadn't noticed Him!

My life wasn't the only one that was dramatically changed, however. My daughter Abigail's life has "exploded". Abi wrote my testimony as she experienced it in high school, which is when the event happened. Now Abi is in her thirties, the mother of three little boys, age four and under. She has journeyed through high school, college, working as a manager at The Outback Steakhouse, ministering on a mission trip to China, and later as an agent for the FBI...eventually falling in love and marrying. What is doubly amazing is that this was a daughter who had decided that she didn't want to marry, and would never dream of having children – it is so funny how living your life for the Lord can change your mind, your desires, your attitude, and your plans!

The story of the teddy bear never grows old, never fails to bring chills and never, ever, appears less than a miracle:

It was a typical Sunday morning. My mother was driving me to Wellington High School, where New Community Church held their services. I was fifteen and only had a driver's permit so this chauffeuring happened to be the normal scenario. Of course, my mother and I went through the regular routine: I invited her to come to church with me, she responded as usual with "work this" or "busy that." I didn't actually wait for a reply as I was already thinking of my next question: when would she pick me up? This Sunday wasn't much different. She was showing property to someone and would try to come back for me around noon. We left it at that.

We were both caught up in our own thoughts when her phone rang for the millionth time that morning and she gave me that apologetic smile as she dug in her bag for the ringing priority. I shifted my gaze out of the right-hand window and casually listened in on her conversation. The radio station was on a commercial break anyway.

"Heeellllooo! This is Jackie Nairnsey. How may I help you?" Her English accent is always strongest at the beginning of her conversations, and this one was no exception.

She listened intently and then the smile in her voice dropped and her tone dampened. The unexpected had happened; her clients had canceled their appointment. As I overheard this change of events, a triumphant smile spread across my face. I looked at my mother at the exact moment she looked at me and she realized she now had no excuse for skipping the church service.

Now, you must understand something. Growing up, my family was never what you would call "church going." I never attended a single service until my 8th grade year, and as my mother has since told me, she hadn't been to church for over thirty five years. So this opening in my mother's busy schedule was a rather convenient snatch of serendipity for me, and a rather disturbing inconvenience for her. There was no getting out of this predicament!

I didn't need to say a word, my satisfied smile said it all and I just directed my mother to a parking spot. We got out and headed towards the entrance of the high school. There were the usual greeters and friendly faces and I still wore that wall-to-wall smile as I led my entrapped mother into the little theater where the service took place.

When we arrived at the theater doors, being the loving and comforting daughter that I'm NOT, I decided to join my friends sitting to the right of the theater. I left my poor mother standing at the entrance by herself! It seemed like the best thing for me to do at the time. Looking back, of course, I see that such a move was cruel and unusual punishment for a new visitor to a new church. My deserted mother, however, happened to see a familiar face in the crowd. Wanda Smith, fellow real estate agent and a charter member of our friendly congregation, invited my mother to sit with her during the service.

The lights were dimmed and the service started promptly. This particular service started with what we called a "Focus Speaker." Beth Blackwood had been asked to speak on how God had touched her life that past week. Having a Focus Speaker was not a new thing at all. Typically, a member of the church spoke every couple of weeks or so. It was a great way to see God working in our everyday lives and situations.

Well, Beth began by telling us how she had been reading a parenting guide that emphasized how to reward and discipline children by using a consistent and immediate "strict mental mommy process." She then described a typical day in her hectic life – and specifically one that had occurred the week before. On this particular day, her infant was sick with a violent flu and she and two of her four children, the infant and a toddler, were at the pharmacy picking up a prescription to fight the infection. Needless to say, the situation at the pharmacy was chaotic. As Beth was at the register trying to find her wallet in her bag, holding on to the sick baby, and keeping an eye on her wandering toddler, the infant threw up into her bag and all over the counter, causing a distressful scene.

In the midst of the clean-up process, the toddler had found a little teddy bear on display at the front of the store and asked her preoccupied mother if she could have it. Beth, with the parenting guide "mental procedure" at the top of her thoughts, went through the suggested process of weighing the toddler's good deeds with her bad deeds of the day, combined with the reactions of what the other children would think and feel. After running all of these thoughts through her mommy computer, she came up with the simple answer of, "No."

Being caught up with the present clean-up situation, Beth didn't expound on the answer any more than this two-letter response. And the toddler, probably sensing her mother's deep distress, just replaced the small toy without a word of complaint or protest. After the mess was taken care of and the prescription paid for, it was on to the rest of her busy itinerary.

While approaching the door at the front of the pharmacy, Beth was approached by a friendly stranger who was carrying a little paper bag. The stranger introduced herself and explained that she had witnessed the whole drama at the pharmacy and had been very impressed with the little toddler's self-discipline and obedience to her mother. The stranger gave the bag to Beth and said that it was for

GOD LOVES US FOR JUST BEING US
AND HE DOESN'T COMPUTE OUR
GOOD DEEDS AND OUR BAD DEEDS
AND WHAT OTHERS WILL THINK IN
ORDER TO REWARD US.

the toddler, "because sometimes you need to reward a little girl, just for being a little girl." Inside the bag was the little teddy bear that the toddler had found in the display at the front of the store.

This whole situation had stunned Beth and as she concluded her Focus that morning in church, she told us that this gift from a complete stranger reminded her that this is how God loves all of us. He loves us for just being us and He doesn't compute our good deeds and our bad deeds and what others will think in order to reward us.

As Beth walked off the stage, I looked around the theater and saw that we were all, even my mother, touched by her story. As the service continued and we listened to the message I kept an eye on my mother to see her reaction. She seemed distracted and upset and I didn't understand what was wrong. Actually, I started to feel guilty about not sitting with her and wondered who was beside her.

At the end of the service, we filed out. Now truly upset, I searched for my mother to apologize for leaving her, and wanting desperately to introduce her to my friends. When I finally found her, she was a wreck. "What's wrong, Mom? What can I do?" Tears streamed down her face as she raised her head and sobbed: "I am the teddy bear lady."

WITH SUCH AN INTRODUCTION, WHO COULD POSSIBLY DOUBT THAT GOD HAD HIS HAND IN HER LIFE?

It took me a couple of seconds to comprehend what she had just said. The enormity of the situation had to sink in, and I was still struggling to understand it. My mother hadn't been to church for over thirty years and my immediate realization was that without dozens of circumstances falling into the pattern at the right time, she would not have been at church this day either. There were far too many factors in the "mix" to be considered mere coincidences. Being an ardent follower of left-brain thinking and attitude, I know I'd have had a hard time believing this story if it hadn't happened in front of my very eyes.

I feel my mother was the perfect recipient of such a miracle, but the particular way it happened is mind boggling to those of us who witnessed it. With such an introduction, who could possibly doubt that God had had His hand in her life? So it was not surprising that my mother chose to continue to attend New Community Church from that remarkable day on, and that she soon started to understand that a relationship with Jesus is the only way to live one's life. Mother rapidly became a sheep in Jesus' flock and she continues to follow the light of His Path each day.

-- Abigail Nairnsey

"Many are the plans in a man's heart, But it is the Lord's purpose that prevails."
Proverbs 19:22 (NIV)

As I look at the final words of Abi's story, and the scripture she chose, I can't help but reflect on where that walk has taken me! It is nothing short of amazing what the Lord can do with your life, if you just let Him. I feel one of the most important realizations is not even recorded in Abi's story...it was because Abi was befriended by Jenelle, the young girl who first invited her to become a part of the Youth Group that they both loved, that Abi found herself regularly attending New Community Church; paving the way for her mother to become involved at a later stage; and starting the domino reaction of events to follow.

So often our youth become discouraged, thinking they may not be able to make much of a "difference" for the Lord, feeling that they are just children. I bear good witness to the fact that without Jenelle and the wonderful New Community youth group, neither Abi nor I would have become Christians; no five years of Drama Ministry; no *Power of Present Day Parables;* no Miracles and Maggie's Tea Room; no missionary work.

I would not have become involved with the wonderful children at City of Hope in Honduras, nor have the privilege of helping to get the new dormitory built. On top of which, you would not be holding the book you are reading. There seems some irony to the fact that the youth of New Community Church in Wellington have a direct link with helping the youth at City of Hope; other teenagers in the same age group in another country, twenty years on! As my grandsons would say, "How cool is that?"

"Now may the God of peace who brought again from the dead Lord Jesus, the great shepherd of the sheep, by the blood of the eternal covenant, equip you with everything good that you may do His will, working in us that which is pleasing in His sight, through Jesus Christ, to whom be the glory for ever and ever. Amen."
Hebrews 13:20-21 (ESV)

"Unless the Lord builds the house,
those who build it labor in vain."
Psalm 127:1 (ESV)

New Dormitory Construction, February, 2013

"Do not despise these small beginnings,
for the Lord rejoices to see the work begin."
Zechariah 4:10 (NLT)

ABOUT CASA HOGAR, CITY OF HOPE

The City of Hope Orphanage is set high up on a mountain just to the south of Tegucigalpa, in the central region of Honduras. It was established in 1999 by Pastor Jose Inestroza, to provide a nurturing home for abandoned, abused and neglected children of the region.

His vision was not a short term one; it was to take these precious souls and turn their lives completely around, to cherish them and lead them from despair through recovery and on into a happy and meaningful life. It is a vision to give them hope, a purpose and a future using their own God-given passions in order to make a difference to their own home country of Honduras, and perhaps on into the world.

Our present goal is to finish the construction of a desperately needed dormitory in order to be able to separate the boys and girls who are presently sharing one building and a partially functioning bathroom in a building that needs renovation and underpinning.

Ultimately, our goal is to provide hope and a home for even more of God's desperate children.

Please visit us at www.cityofhopehonduras.org.

www.ingramcontent.com/pod-product-compliance
Lightning Source LLC
LaVergne TN
LVHW051632080426
835511LV00016B/2311